Glencoe
EARTH SCIENCE

LABORATORY MANUAL
Student Edition

New York, New York   Columbus, Ohio   Mission Hills, California   Peoria, Illinois

A GLENCOE PROGRAM
Glencoe Earth Science

Student Edition
Teacher Wraparound Edition
Study Guide, SE and TE
Reinforcement, SE and TE
Enrichment, SE and TE
Concept Mapping
Critical Thinking/Problem Solving
Activity Worksheets
Chapter Review
Chapter Review Software
Laboratory Manual, SE and TE
Science Integration Activities

Cross-Curricular Integration
Science and Society Integration
Technology Integration
Multicultural Connections
Performance Assessment
Assessment—Chapter and Unit Tests
Spanish Resources
MindJogger Videoquizzes and Teacher Guide
English/Spanish Audiocassettes
CD-ROM Multimedia System
Interactive Videodisc Program
Computer Test Bank—DOS and Macintosh

Transparency Packages:
   Teaching Transparencies
   Section Focus Transparencies
   Science Integration Transparencies

The Glencoe Science Professional Development Series:
   Performance Assessment in the Science Classroom
   Lab and Safety Skills in the Science Classroom
   Cooperative Learning in the Science Classroom
   Alternate Assessment in the Science Classroom
   Exploring Environmental Issues

Glencoe/McGraw-Hill
A Division of The McGraw-Hill Companies

Copyright © by Glencoe/McGraw-Hill. All rights reserved. Except as permitted under the United States Copyright Act, no part of this publication may be reproduced or distributed in any form or by any means, or stored in a database or retrieval system, without prior permission of the publisher.

Send all inquiries to:
Glencoe/McGraw-Hill
936 Eastwind Drive
Westerville, OH 43081

Printed in the United States of America

ISBN 0-02-827813-5

1 2 3 4 5 6 7 8 9 10 MAL 04 03 02 01 00 99 98 97 96

TO THE STUDENT

Science is the body of information including all the hypotheses and experiments that tell us about our environment. All people involved in scientific work use similar methods for gaining information. One important scientific skill is the ability to obtain data directly from the environment. Observations must be based on what actually happens in the environment. Equally important is the ability to organize this data into a form from which valid conclusions can be drawn. The conclusions must be such that other scientists can achieve the same results.

Glencoe Earth Science: Laboratory Manual is designed for your active participation. The activities in this manual require testing hypotheses, applying known data, discovering new information, and drawing conclusions from observed results. You will be performing activities using the same processes that professional scientists use. Work slowly and record as many observations and as much numerical data as possible. You will often be instructed to make tables and graphs to organize your data. Using these tools, you will be able to explain ideas more clearly and accurately.

Each activity in *Glencoe Earth Science: Laboratory Manual* is designed to guide you in the processes scientists use to solve a problem. The **Introduction** provides information about the problem under study. The **Strategy** tells you what you are expected to learn from the activity. These statements emphasize the most important concept(s) in the activity. **Materials** tells you the equipment and supplies needed to conduct the activity. **Procedure** is the list of steps you follow in doing the activity. **Data and Observations** is the section in which you record your findings. Record all observations, no matter how minor they may seem. In some activities, you will be asked to organize your data into tables or graphs. Organizing data helps you recognize relationships among the data. In **Questions and Conclusions,** you must give written answers to questions and problems. The questions are designed to test your understanding of the purpose and results of the activity. The last section is the **Strategy Check.** If you can answer "yes" to each question, you understand the concepts involved in the activity. If not, reread or repeat the activity to see if you can identify the concept you do not understand.

Remember that the way you approach a problem—collecting data and making observations—is as important as the "right" answer. Good luck in your laboratory experiences.

TABLE OF CONTENTS

Laboratory Equipment vii

Laboratory Techniques ix

Safety Symbols xii

Unit 1   Earth Materials

1. Problem Solving and the Scientific Method 1
2. The Law of Probability 3
3. Measuring Using SI Units 7
4. Mass and Weight 9
5. Mixtures and Compounds 11
6. Ions 13
7. Electrical Charges 15
8. Density and Buoyancy 17
9. States of Matter 19
10. Crystal Formation 21
11. Minerals and Optical Crystallography 25
12. Mineral Resources 27
13. Removal of Waste Rock 29
14. Gas Production in Magma 31
15. Metamorphic Processes 33
16. Concretions 35

Unit 2   The Changing Surface of Earth

17. Determining Latitude 37
18. Time Zones 41
19. Comparing Maps 43
20. Using a Clinometer 47
21. Chemical Weathering 51
22. Soil Infiltration by Groundwater 53
23. Mass Movements 55
24. Model Glacier 57
25. Transporting Soil Materials by Runoff 59
26. Capillary Action 61
27. Carbon Dioxide and Limestone 63
28. Waves, Currents, and Coastal Features 65
29. Earthquakes 69

Unit 3   Earth's Internal Processes

30. Locating an Earthquake 73
31. Effect of Magma on Surrounding Rock 77
32. Volcanic Preservation 79
33. Continental Drift 81

Unit 4   Change and Earth's History

34. Principle of Superposition 85
35. Carbon Impressions 89

TABLE OF CONTENTS *(continued)*

    36. Geologic Time 91
    37. Differences in a Species 95

Unit 5   Earth's Air and Water

    38. Air 97
    39. Air Pressure 99
    40. Temperature of the Air 101
    41. Air in Motion 103
    42. Wind Power 105
    43. Clouds 109
    44. Hurricanes 111
    45. Weather Forecasting 115
    46. Radiant Energy and Climate 117
    47. Solar Energy Storage 119
    48. Solar Energy Application 121
    49. Salt Concentration in Ocean Water 125
    50. Fresh Water from Ocean Water 127
    51. Density Currents 129
    52. Floating in Fresh Water and in Ocean Water 131
    53. Mapping the Ocean Floor 133

Unit 6   You and the Environment

    54. Human Impact on the Environment 135
    55. Reclamation of Mine Wastes 139
    56. Conservation—Recycling 141
    57. Smoke Pollution 143
    58. Water Purification 147

Unit 7   Astronomy

    59. Refraction of Light 149
    60. Spectral Analysis 151
    61. Earth's Spin 155
    62. Earth's Magnetism 157
    63. Moon Phases 159
    64. Newton's First Law of Motion 161
    65. Venus—The Greenhouse Effect 163
    66. Jupiter and Its Moons 167
    67. Astronomical Distances 169
    68. Star Colors 171
    69. Star Trails 173
    70. Star Positions 175

LABORATORY EQUIPMENT

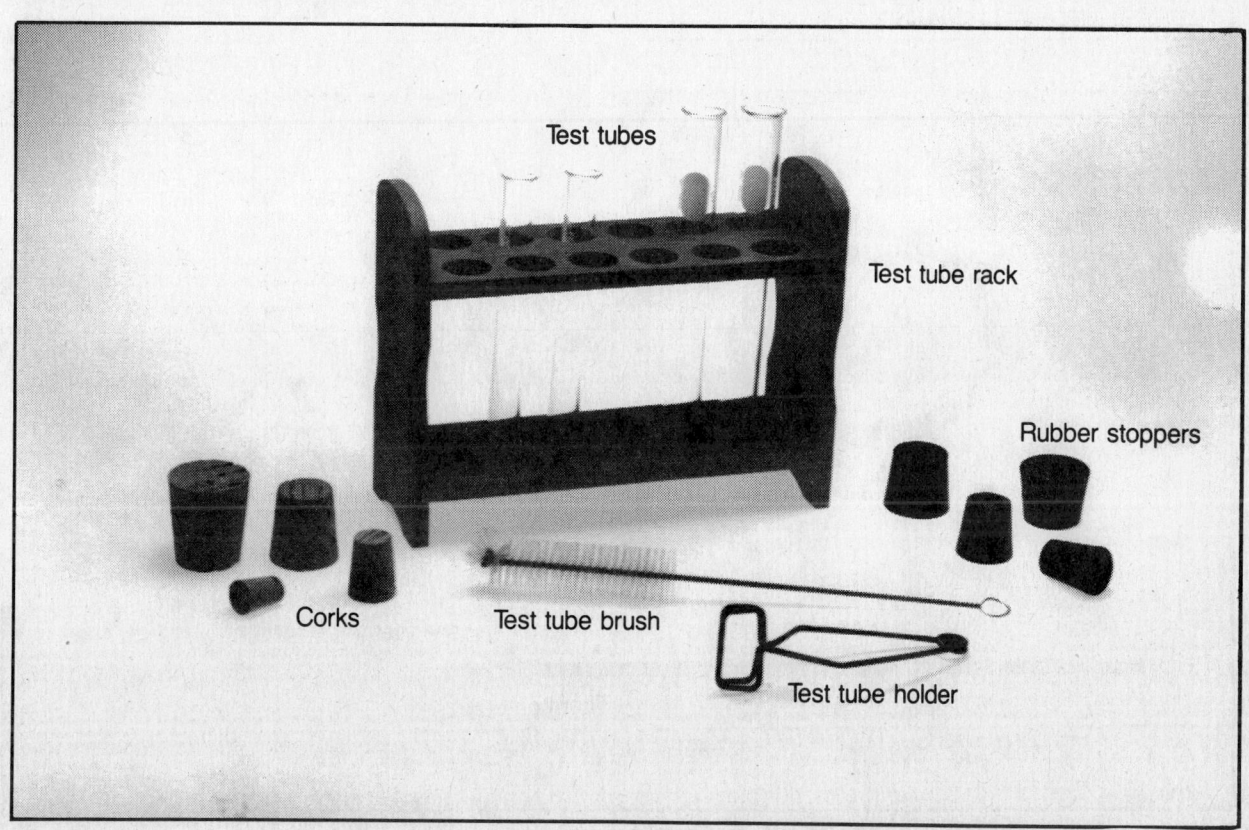

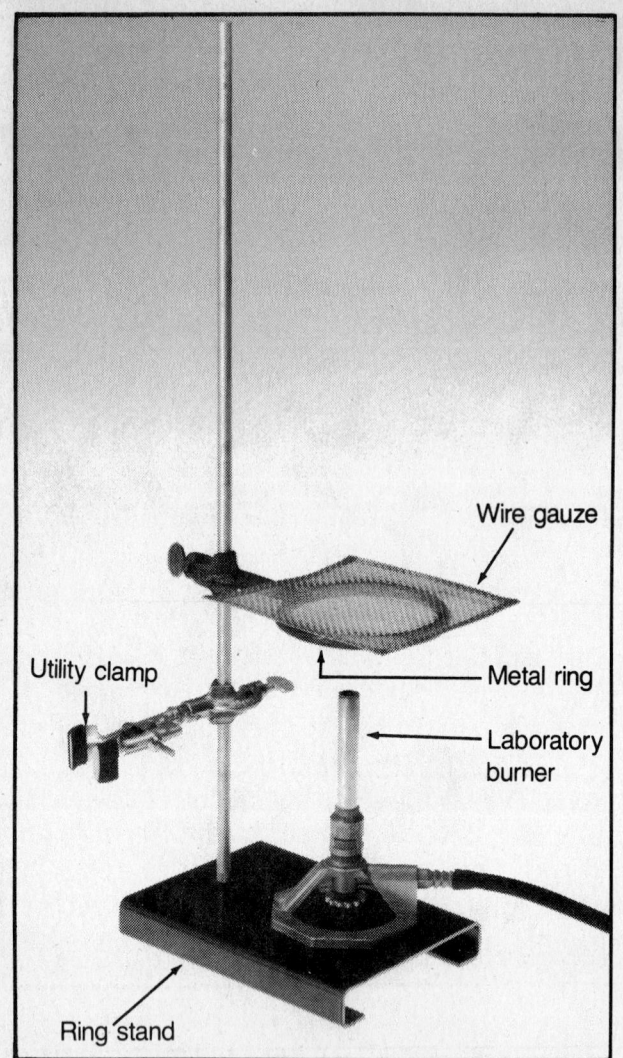
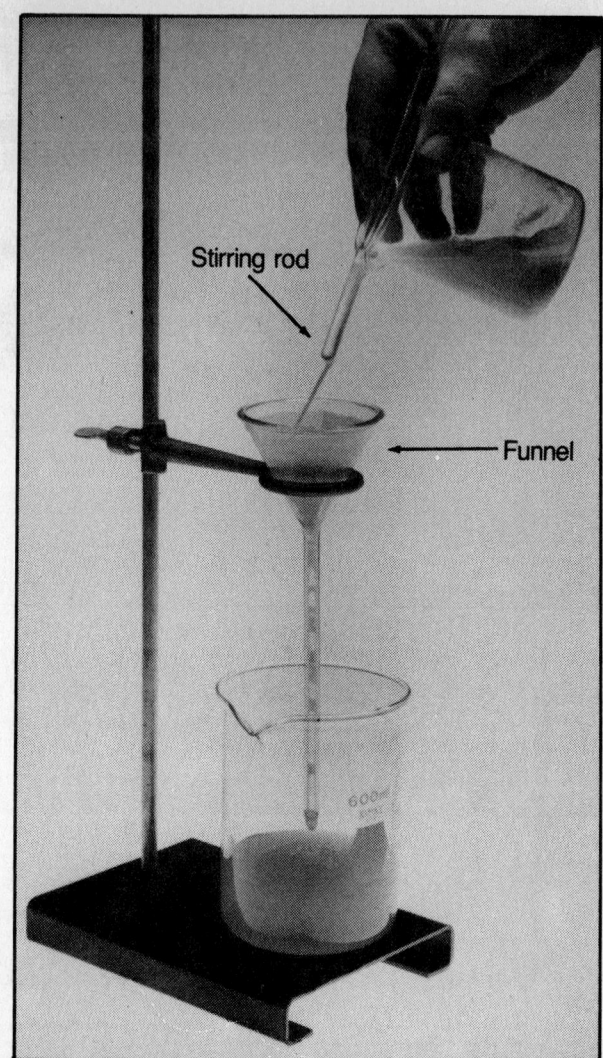
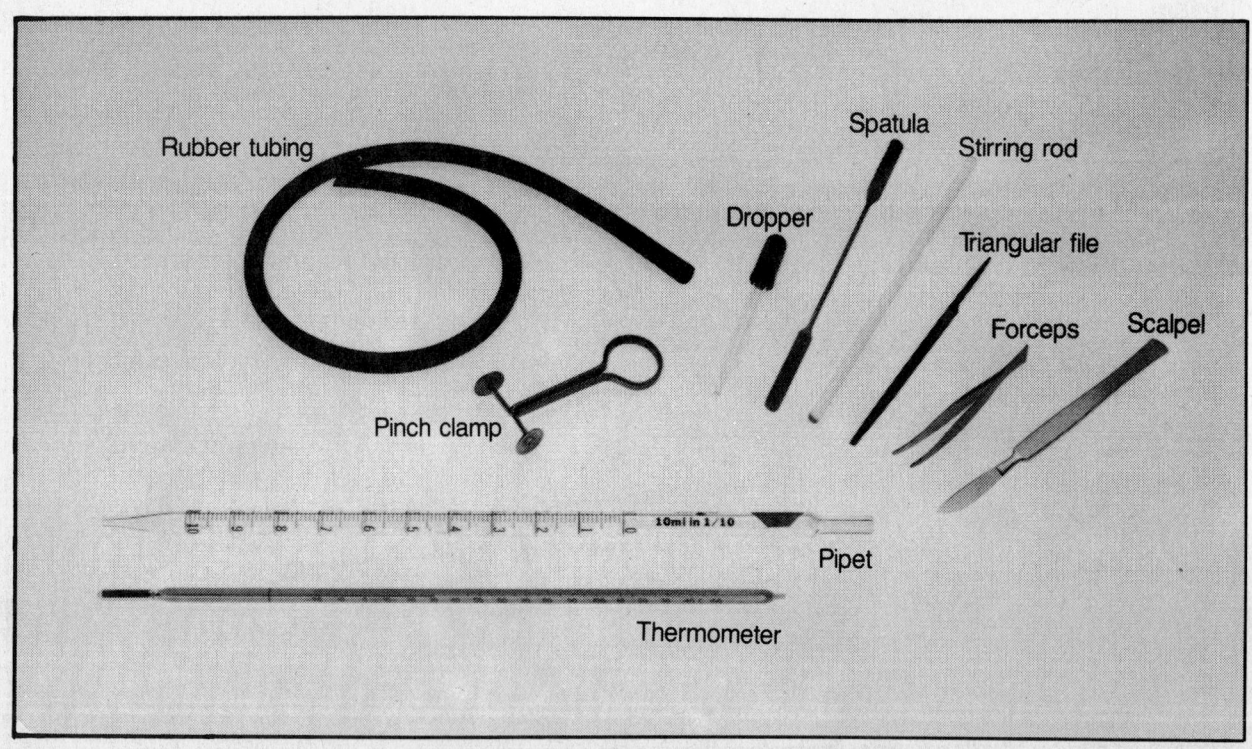

LABORATORY TECHNIQUES

Lighting a Laboratory Burner and Adjusting the Flame

Connect the hose of the burner to a gas supply. Partly open the valve on the gas supply, and hold a lighted match to the edge of the top of the burner. See Figure A.

The size of the flame can be changed by opening and closing the valve on the gas supply. The color of the flame indicates the amount of air in the gas. The air supply is controlled by moving the tube of the burner. A yellow flame indicates more air is needed, and the burner tube can be turned to increase the amount of air. If the flame goes out, the air supply should be reduced by turning the burner tube in the opposite direction. The gas supply is controlled by the valve on the bottom of the burner. The hottest part of the flame is just above the tip of the inner cone of the flame.

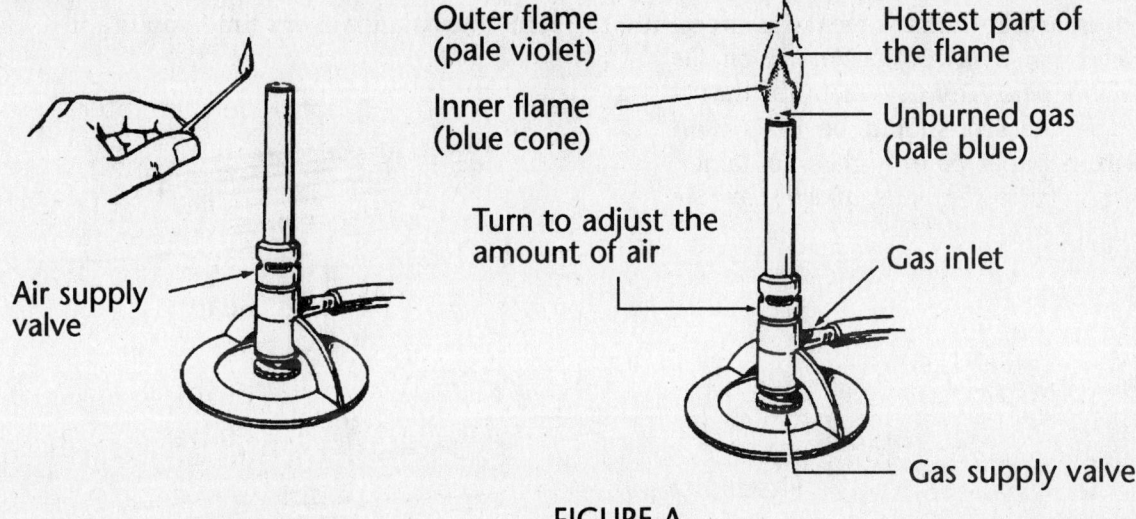

FIGURE A

Decanting and Filtering

It is often necessary to separate a solid from a liquid. Filtration is a common process of separation used in most laboratories. The liquid is decanted, that is, the liquid is separated from the solid by carefully pouring off the liquid leaving only the solid material. To avoid splashing and to maintain control, the liquid is poured down a stirring rod. See Figure B. The solution is usually filtered through filter paper to catch any solid that has not settled to the bottom of the beaker. See Figure C.

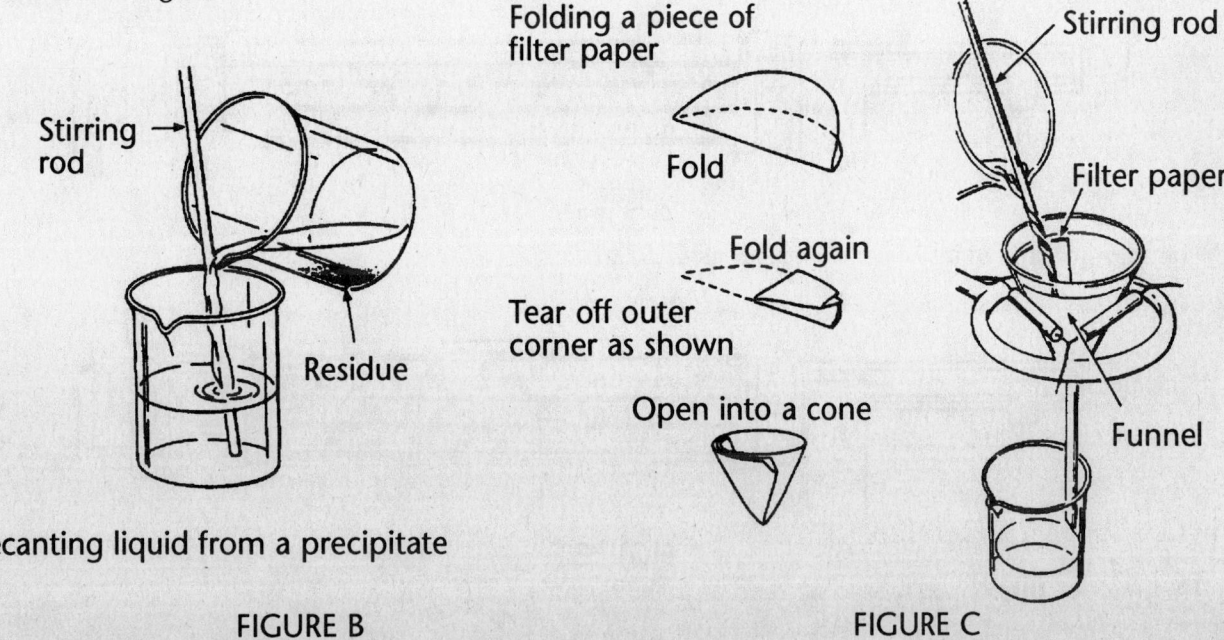

Decanting liquid from a precipitate

FIGURE B   FIGURE C

ix

Using the Balance

There are various types of laboratory balances in common use today. The balance you use may look somewhat different from the one in Figure D; however, all beam balances have some common features. The following technique should be used in transporting a balance.

(1) Be sure all riders are back to the zero point.
(2) If the balance has a lock mechanism to lock the pan(s), be sure it is on.
(3) Place one hand under the balance and the other hand on the beam's support.

The following steps should be followed in using the balance.

(1) Before determining the mass of any substance, slide all of the riders back to the zero point. Check to see that the pointer swings freely along the scale. You do not have to wait for the pointer to stop at the zero point. The beam should swing an equal distance above and below the zero point. Use the adjustment screw to obtain an equal swing of the beams, if necessary. You must repeat this procedure to "zero" the balance every time you use it.

(2) *Never put a hot object directly on the balance pan.* Any dry chemical that is to be massed should be placed on waxed paper or in a glass container. *Never pour chemicals directly on the balance pan.*

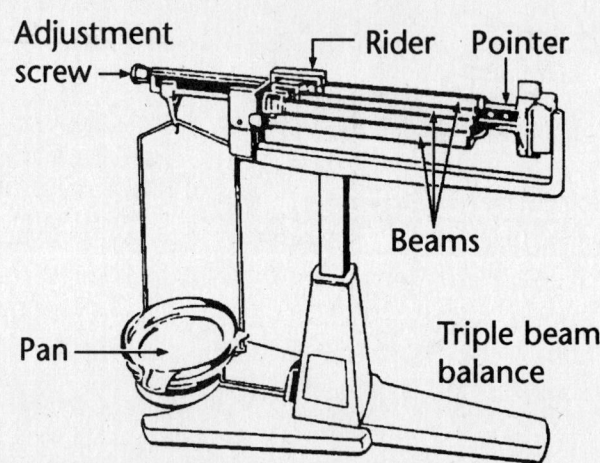

FIGURE D

(3) Once you have placed the object to be massed on the pan, move the riders along the beams beginning with the largest mass first. If the beams are notched, make sure all riders are in a notch before you take a reading. Remember, the pointer does not have to stop swinging, but the swing should be an equal distance above and below the zero point on the scale.

(4) The mass of the object will be the sum of the masses indicated on the beams. For example:

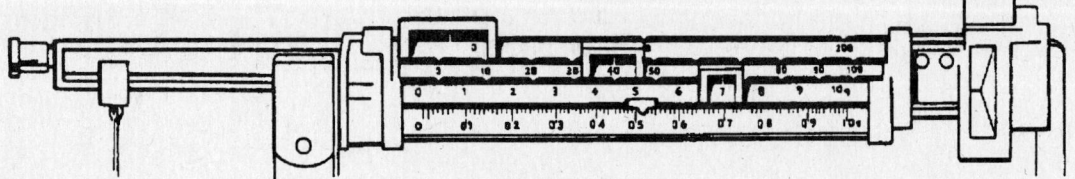

FIGURE E

The mass of this object would be read as 47.52 grams.

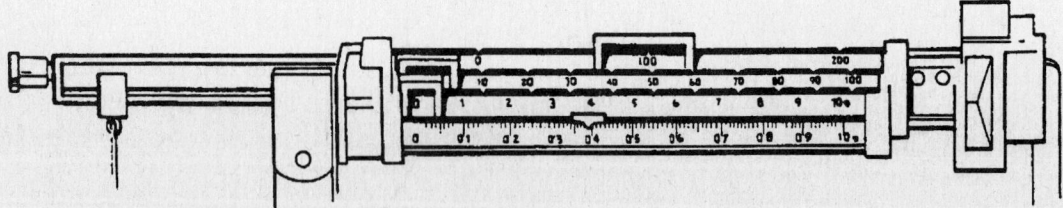

FIGURE F

The mass of this object would be read as 100.39 grams.

Measuring Temperature

When the temperature of a liquid is measured with a thermometer, the bulb of the thermometer should be in the liquid. When the thermometer is removed from the liquid, the column of mercury or alcohol in the thermometer soon shows the temperature of the air. When measuring the temperature of hot liquids, be sure you use a thermometer that is calibrated for high temperatures.

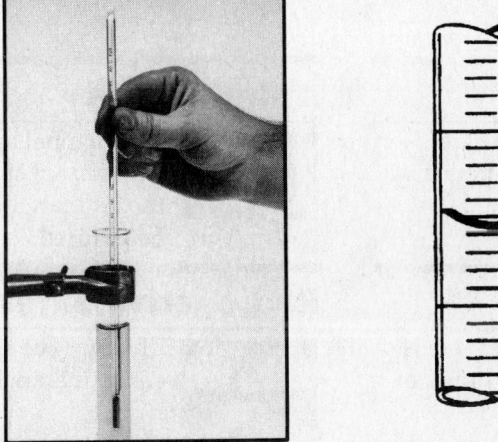

FIGURE G
Measuring temperature

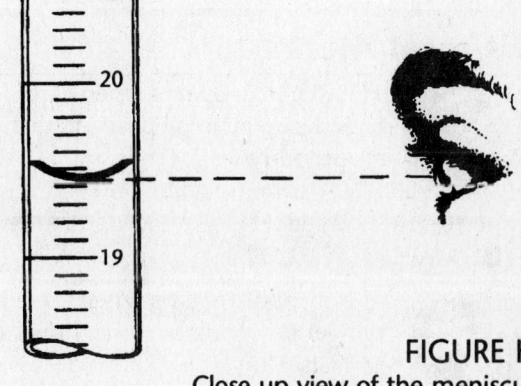

FIGURE H
Close up view of the meniscus

Measuring Volumes

The surface of liquids when viewed in glass cylinders is always curved. This curved surface is called the meniscus. Most of the liquids you will be measuring will have a concave meniscus.

(1) The meniscus must be viewed along a horizontal line of sight. Do not try to make a reading looking up or down at the meniscus. Hold the apparatus up so that its sides are at a right angle to your eye.

(2) Always read a concave meniscus from the bottom. This measurement gives the most precise volume, because the liquid tends to creep up the sides of a glass container. Liquid in many plastic cylinders does not form a meniscus. If you are using a plastic graduate and no meniscus is noticeable, read the volume from the level of the liquid.

Inserting Glass Tubing or a Thermometer into a Stopper

This procedure can be dangerous if you are not careful. Check the size of the holes in the rubber stopper to see if they are just slightly smaller than the glass tubing. The rubber stopper should stretch enough to hold the glass tubing firmly.

Place a drop of glycerol or some water on the end of the glass tubing. Glycerol acts as a lubricant to help make the tubing go through the stopper more easily. Wrap the glass tubing and the stopper in a towel. Then push the tubing through the stopper using a gentle force and a twisting motion. Your hands should not be more than one centimeter apart. *Never* hold the tubing or stopper in such a way that the end of the tubing is pointed toward or pushing against the palm of your hand. If the tubing breaks, you can injure your hand if it is held this way.

This procedure also is used in inserting thermometers in rubber stoppers. Equal caution should be taken.

xi

SAFETY SYMBOLS

These safety symbols are used to indicate possible hazards in the activities. Each activity has appropriate hazard indicators.

Disposal Alert
 This symbol appears when care must be taken to dispose of materials properly.

Biological Hazard
 This symbol appears when there is danger involving bacteria, fungi, or protists.

Open Flame Alert
 This symbol appears when use of an open flame could cause a fire or an explosion.

Thermal Safety
 This symbol appears as a reminder to use caution when handling hot objects.

Sharp Object Safety
 This symbol appears when a danger of cuts or punctures caused by the use of sharp objects exists.

Fume Safety
 This symbol appears when chemicals or chemical reactions could cause dangerous fumes.

Electrical Safety
 This symbol appears when care should be taken when using electrical equipment.

Plant Safety
 This symbol appears when poisonous plants or plants with thorns are handled.

Animal Safety
 This symbol appears whenever live animals are studied and the safety of the animals and the students must be ensured.

Radioactive Safety
 This symbol appears when radioactive materials are used.

Clothing Protection Safety
 This symbol appears when substances used could stain or burn clothing.

Fire Safety
 This symbol appears when care should be taken around open flames.

Explosion Safety
 This symbol appears when the misuse of chemicals could cause an explosion.

Eye Safety
 This symbol appears when a danger to the eyes exists. Safety goggles should be worn when this symbol appears.

Poison Safety
 This symbol appears when poisonous substances are used.

Chemical Safety
 This symbol appears when chemicals used can cause burns or are poisonous if absorbed through the skin.

NAME _____ DATE _____ CLASS _____

Chapter 1
LABORATORY MANUAL

Problem Solving and the Scientific Method 1

Think back to the last problem you had to solve. No matter how you solved the problem, you probably used some or all of the steps of the "Scientific Method." The scientific method is a logical approach to solving problems. There are many methods used by scientists to solve problems. However, most scientists recognize four basic steps: (1) determining the problem, (2) testing, (3) analyzing the results, and (4) drawing conclusions.

Strategy
You will use the scientific method to determine the density of an ice cube.

Materials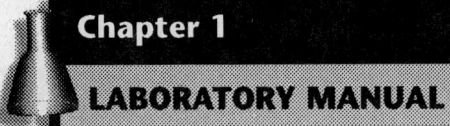
ice cubes   water   graduated beaker
balance   alcohol   forceps or tongs
metric ruler   graduated cylinder stirring rods

Procedure
1. In order to solve the problem, you must first determine what it is you need to know. Place an ice cube on the tabletop and make some observations. It is best to organize your initial observations into a data table for easy review. Now fill out Table 1-1 below.

Data and Observations
Table 1-1

Ice Cube	Observation
A. View on tabletop for five minutes.	
B. Shape	
C. Size	
D. In water	
E. In alcohol	

2. What other information is helpful that cannot be gained from initial observation? A little research might be helpful at this time. Your closest source of information is your textbook.
   A. Define the unknown terms

   Density _____
   Mass   _____
   Volume _____

Copyright © Glencoe/McGraw-Hill, a division of The McGraw-Hill Companies, Inc.

1

3. Design a test (in this case a procedure) that will enable you to determine the density of an ice cube.

First Trial Procedure	Second Trial Procedure (with modifications if necessary)
A. _____	A. _____
B. _____	B. _____
C. _____	C. _____
D. _____	D. _____
E. _____	E. _____

Data collected (framework for writing results)

A. Volume of the ice cube _____ cubic centimeters (cm³)

B. Mass of the ice cube _____ grams (g)

C. Density of the ice cube _____ grams/cubic centimeter (g/cm³)

4. Analyze the results

   A. My answer for the density of the ice cube was _____ .

   B. The accepted value for the density of the ice cube is _____ .

   C. Now determine the percent error. The percent error is determined by the following formula: Accepted Value minus Calculated Value divided by the Accepted Value times 100.

   $$\frac{\text{Accepted} - \text{Calculated}}{\text{Accepted}} \times 100$$

   D. The percent error is _____ .

5. *Conclusion*
   If your percent error is low (under 10%), then your experimental design is acceptable given the materials and the time you had available for completing the task. Knowing the "right" answer to a problem is not always possible. A scientist has to repeat the experiment several times and often will compare the results with others.

6. Did you compare your results with the other students? _____

   _____

   Did you compare procedures? _____

   Do you think you need to modify your procedures? _____

   What is your conclusion? _____

Strategy Check

_____ Can you use the scientific method to determine the density of an ice cube?

NAME _____ DATE _____ CLASS _____

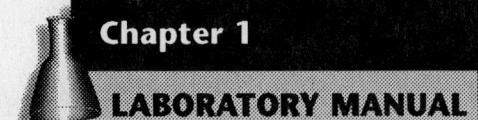

Chapter 1
LABORATORY MANUAL
The Law of Probability 2

Crystals in rocks and cells in plants and animals develop in relatively predictable ways. Other materials behave in unpredictable ways. Gas particles are examples of unpredictable behavior. They move in every direction, bump into obstacles, then fly off in different directions. Scientists make educated guesses about this type of behavior based on the law of probability. They make many observations of the random behavior and find the average of all these observations. They use this average to make predictions about how the material is likely to behave in the future.

Strategy
You will use a spinner to determine the direction and distance you will move.
You will use the law of probability to interpret your random movements.

Materials
cardboard (thin)   pencils (colored)
glue or paste   scissors
graph paper   shirt button
metric ruler   straight pin

Procedure
1. Paste the spinner and pointer section, Figure 2-1, to the cardboard.
2. Cut out the spinner and the pointer.
3. Push the straight pin upward through the center dot of the spinner.
4. Place the button on the pin and then push the pin through the center of the arrow.
5. Spin the arrow. When it stops, read from the outer dial the direction in which you are to move. Record the direction in Table 2-1 on page 4.
6. Spin the arrow again. When it stops, read the number of spaces you are to move from the inner dial. Record the number of spaces in Table 2-1.
7. Record 20 turns (2 spins each turn). This is Trial 1.
8. Spin 20 more turns; record under Trial 2. Spin 20 more turns; record under Trial 3.
9. Start at Point A at the center of the graph paper, and plot your movements for Trial 1. Move diagonally if the direction is northeast, southeast, northwest, or southwest. Move along a grid line if the direction is north, south, east, or west.
10. Using different colored pencils, plot your movements for Trials 2 and 3. Begin plotting each trial at A.
11. Measure the distances along a straight line from A to the end of your random paths. Record. Record the class average also.

Data and Observations

Table 2-1

Turns	Trial 1 Direction	Trial 1 Spaces	Trial 2 Direction	Trial 2 Spaces	Trial 3 Direction	Trial 3 Spaces
1						
2						
3						
4						
5						
6						
7						
8						
9						
10						
11						
12						
13						
14						
15						
16						
17						
18						
19						
20						

Questions and Conclusions

1. Were the three distances equal? _____ Did all three paths follow the same direction? _____

2. Based on your three trials, can you make an accurate prediction of the distance and direction of future paths? _____

| NAME | DATE | CLASS |

3. Would the average distance of 10 paths be more accurate for predicting distance and direction than the average of your three paths? _____ Why? _____
_____

4. How does the class average compare to your average? _____

5. Which is the better prediction, the class average or your average? _____
Why? _____

6. Is a scientific law based on the "law of probability" necessarily incorrect? _____

Strategy Check

____ Can you predict how far from Point A you will travel based on your three paths?

____ Can you predict random motion using the law of probability?

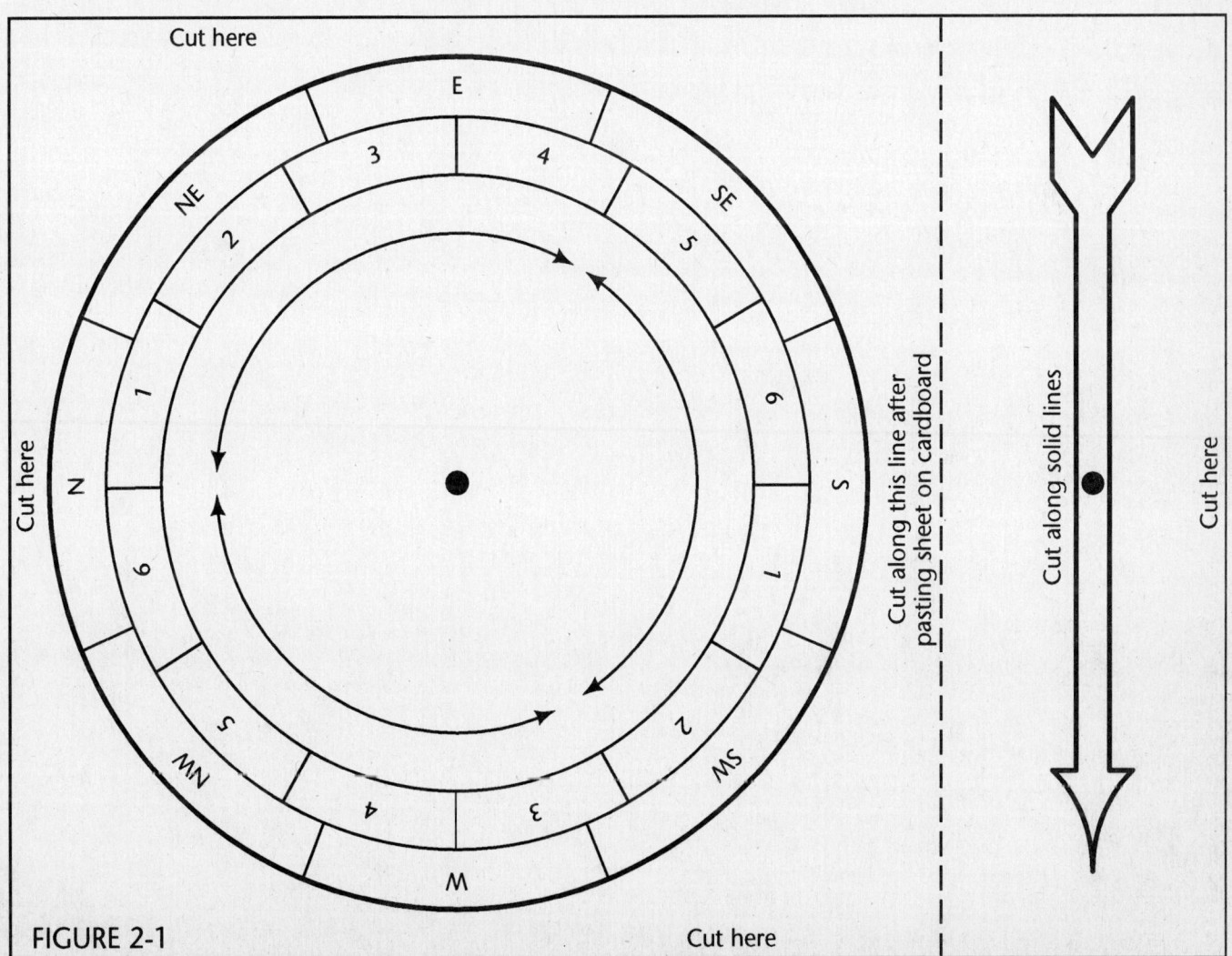

FIGURE 2-1

NAME _____ DATE _____ CLASS _____

Chapter 1

LABORATORY MANUAL

Measuring Using SI Units 3

International System (Système Internationale, or SI) units of measuring are used in science throughout the world. These units are easier to use than our Standard English system of inches, feet, miles, ounces, and pounds. The International System of measures is a decimal system. SI units are based on 10 and multiples of 10. Measuring devices based on SI units include metric rulers, metersticks, liter beakers, and balances graduated in grams and milligrams.

Strategy
You will create a set of masses.
You will use the water displacement method to determine the volumes of the masses.

Materials
balance   clay   materials for creative mass set
beaker (50 mL)   masses (standard set)   water

Procedure
1. Using the balance, measure exactly 10 grams of clay. Mold the clay into any shape.

2. Determine the volume of the clay and record in Table 3-1 on page 8. Sketch the shape of the mass and set the mass aside. Record all data in the table.

3. Using one of the materials provided by the teacher, make a set of masses. You should have five 1-gram masses; two 2-gram masses; one 5-gram mass; one 10-gram mass; and one 20-gram mass. Record the materials you choose.

4. When you have created your set of masses, use the balance to see if the 20-gram mass exactly balances the combined masses of the 10-gram mass, two 2-gram masses, one 5-gram mass, and one 1-gram mass. Record your results in the table.

5. Determine the volume of each mass of your set. Record in the table.

Data and Observations (See page 8.)

Questions and Conclusions
1. Do the sums of the masses exactly equal 20 grams? _____
   _____

2. What materials did you use? _____ What were some of the problems you
   encountered in using these materials? _____
   _____

3. How accurate is your set of masses? _____
   _____
   _____

Copyright © Glencoe/McGraw-Hill, a division of the McGraw-Hill Companies, Inc.

4. How did you determine the volume of each of the masses? _____
_____

5. Do all the 10-gram clay masses have the same volume regardless of shape? _____
   Do all the 10-gram masses of the class have the same volume? _____
   Explain. _____
   _____

6. Why do you think the shape of the standard masses was chosen? _____
   _____

7. Why do you think brass was chosen as the material used to make the standard masses?
   _____
   _____
   _____
   _____

Table 3-1

Material used	Mass (g)	Volume (mL)
Clay	10	
	1	
	5	
	10	
	20	
Masses balance?	Yes ☐	No ☐

Sketch mass here.

Strategy Check

_____ Can you create a set of masses?

_____ Can you use the water displacement method to determine the volume of masses?

8   Copyright © Glencoe/McGraw-Hill, a division of the McGraw-Hill Companies, Inc.

NAME _____ DATE _____ CLASS _____

Chapter 1
LABORATORY MANUAL

● Mass and Weight 4

Mass is the measure of the amount of matter in an object. Weight is the measure of the force with which one body is attracted toward another body. This force of attraction is called gravity. For example, the moon is attracted toward Earth by Earth's gravity field. Likewise, Earth is attracted toward the moon by the moon's gravity field.

Strategy
You will measure the force of gravity on marbles.
You will deduce the relationship between mass and weight.

Materials
balance
12 glass marbles (large)
meterstick
plastic bottle (with handle)
rubber band (large, wide)

Procedure
1. Cut the rubber band. Attach one end to the handle of the bottle.

2. Measure the mass of the bottle and the attached rubber band in grams and record in Table 4-1. Lift the bottle using the rubber band. Measure the length of the rubber band in centimeters and record.

3. Place three marbles in the bottle. Measure the mass of the bottle with the three marbles in it and record. Lift the bottle. Measure the length of the rubber band in centimeters and record.

4. Add three more marbles to the bottle and measure the mass of the bottle with the six marbles in it. Record in the table. Lift the bottle and measure the length of the rubber band. Record.

5. Add the remaining marbles and measure the mass of the bottle with the twelve marbles in it. Record. Lift the bottle, measure the length of the rubber band, and record.

Data and Observations
Table 4-1

	Mass (g)	Length of the rubber band (cm)
Plastic bottle		
Bottle + 3 marbles		
Bottle + 6 marbles		
Bottle + 12 marbles		

Questions and Conclusions

1. What did the rubber band represent? _____

2. What two objects were attracting each other? _____

3. What happened to the mass of the plastic bottle and its contents as you added marbles?
   _____

4. What happened to the length of the rubber band as you added more mass to the plastic bottle?
   _____
   _____

5. What happened to the force of attraction between Earth and the plastic bottle and its contents?
   _____
   _____

6. How are mass and weight related? _____
   _____
   _____

7. If the force of attraction (gravity) on the moon is 1/6 that of the force on Earth, what would you weigh on the moon if you weighed 42 kilograms, or about 412 N (newtons)? _____
   _____
   _____

8. If your mass on Earth were 42 kilograms, what would your mass be on the moon? _____
   _____

Strategy Check

____ Can you measure the force of gravity on marbles?

____ Can you state the relationship between mass and weight?

NAME _____ DATE _____ CLASS _____

Chapter 2

LABORATORY MANUAL • **Mixtures and Compounds 5**

Matter is anything that has mass and occupies space. Matter exists in different forms. Three forms of matter are well known to us; elements, mixtures, and compounds. Elements are the basic materials of our world. Elements in a mixture have recognizable boundaries and can be separated by mechanical means. Elements that form a chemical compound can be separated only by a chemical process. Oxygen (O) is an element, which combined with hydrogen forms water, H_2O, a compound. Salt water is a mixture of two compounds, water and salt.

Strategy
You will separate a mixture into its parts.
You will compare the characteristics of a compound and a mixture.

Materials

| granite | heat source | 2 pie pans (disposable) | sand (coarse) |
| granite (crushed) | magnifying glass | rock salt | water |

Procedure

1. Use the magnifying glass to observe the sand and granite. Sketch the shapes of the different minerals found in the granite and the shapes of the sand grains under Sketch A.

2. Sort the crushed granite into separate piles according to color.

3. Sketch the general shape of a piece from each pile of the sorted granite and label it as to color under Sketch B.

4. Mix a spoonful of sand in some water in a pie pan. Sketch what you observed under Sketch C.

5. Examine and sketch the salt crystals under Sketch D.

6. Mix a spoonful of salt in some water in the second pie pan. Record your observations.

7. Heat both pans until the water is evaporated. Sketch what is left in each pan under Sketch E.
   CAUTION: *Be careful not to get clothes or hair close to the heat source.*

Data and Observations

Sketch A

Sketch B

Sketch C

Sketch D

Sketch E

Questions and Conclusions

1. Are any of the sand grains similar to any of the granite fragments? _____
   If so, describe them. _____
   _____

2. How are salt and sand similar? _____
   How are they different? _____

3. Is salt water a compound or mixture? _____ Explain. _____
   _____
   _____

4. Is granite a compound or mixture? _____ Explain. _____
   _____
   _____

5. Name some mechanical processes used to separate mixtures. _____
   _____
   _____

Strategy Check

____ Can you separate components of a mixture?

____ Can you tell the difference between a compound and a mixture?

NAME　　　　　　　　　　　　　　DATE　　　　　　　　　　　　　CLASS

Chapter 2
LABORATORY MANUAL
Ions 6

Although the mass of an electron is smaller than that of a proton or a neutron, the electron controls the chemical properties of the atom. An atom has an equal number of positively charged protons and negatively charged electrons. Thus, an atom is electrically neutral or balanced. If an atom loses or gains electrons, it is called an ion. An ion is positively charged if an electron has been lost; negatively charged if an electron has been gained. Ions with opposite charges combined chemically to form molecules. Compounds that contain a large number of positive hydrogen ions are called acids. Compounds called bases combine easily with hydrogen ions.

Strategy
You will test for positive ions.
You will test for negative ions.
You will observe the combination of positive and negative ions into a neutral compound.

Materials

ammonia water	dropper	litmus paper (red and blue or phenolphthalein)
apron	goggles	stirring rod
2 beakers (100 mL)	graduated cylinder (50 mL)	vinegar (white)

Procedure

1. Pour 20 mL of ammonia water into a beaker. **CAUTION:** *Avoid contact with skin. Vapors are irritating to the eyes and lungs.* Test the ammonia water with a strip of red litmus and a strip of blue litmus. Record your observations in Table 6-1.

2. Pour 20 mL of vinegar into the second beaker. Test the vinegar with both red and blue litmus. Record your observations.

3. Slowly add the vinegar to the ammonia water using the dropper. Stir gently with the stirring rod.

4. Test this liquid with both red and blue litmus after each addition of vinegar. Record your observations.

Data and Observations

Table 6-1

Liquid	Red litmus	Blue litmus	Other observations

Copyright © Glencoe/McGraw-Hill, a division of the McGraw-Hill Companies, Inc.

13

Questions and Conclusions

1. Litmus paper is an indicator of acids and bases. Litmus turns blue in a base and red in an acid.

    (a) Based on your observations, ammonia water is a(n) _____

    (b) Based on your observations, vinegar is a(n) _____

2. What type of ions does vinegar contain? _____ Explain. _____
   _____
   _____

3. What occurred when you mixed ammonia water and the vinegar? _____
   _____
   _____

4. Do you think this was a chemical or physical reaction? _____
   Explain. _____
   _____
   _____
   _____

Strategy Check

____ Can you test for positive ions?

____ Can you test for negative ions?

____ Can you test for the combination of positive and negative ions?

| NAME | DATE | CLASS |

Chapter 2
LABORATORY MANUAL
● Electrical Charges 7

In 1733, a French investigator, DuFay, found that all substances with electrical charges behave either like glass, which DuFay called positive, or like hard rubber, which DuFay called negative. Rubbing glass and rubber with silk or wool causes the glass to lose electrons and rubber to gain electrons. Similarly charged bodies repel one another; oppositely charged bodies attract one another. Friction causes the substances rubbed together to gain opposite electrical charges. Thus, silk or wool may be positive if used to rub hard rubber; negative if used to rub glass.

Strategy
You will use friction to produce electrical charges.
You will demonstrate that opposite electrical charges attract while similar electrical charges repel.

Materials
2 balloons   glass stirring rod   water
silk scarf   string, 70 cm

Procedure
1. Blow up the balloons. Tie a balloon at each end of the piece of string.
2. Rub each balloon with the silk. Hold the string in the center and let the balloons hang free.
3. Record your observations under Sketch A.
4. Cut the string close to one balloon.
5. Rub the balloon with the silk again. Place the balloon on the floor.
6. Let the silk touch the balloon. Lift the balloon as high as possible.
7. Turn on the water in the sink. Let it run in a gentle stream.
8. Rub the stirring rod with the silk. Bring the glass close to the stream of water. Record your observations under Observations B.

Data and Observations

Sketch A

Observations B:

_____
_____
_____
_____

Questions and Conclusions

1. If the scarf gains electrons from the balloons, what kind of electrical charge does the scarf have?
_____

2. What kind of electrical charge do the balloons have? _____

3. Why do the balloons repel each other? _____

4. Why can you pick up the balloon with the scarf? _____
_____
_____

5. What electrical charge did the glass rod have after it was rubbed with silk? _____

6. What happened to the stream of water when the glass rod was brought close to the water?
_____

   Explain. _____
_____
_____

7. When you walk across a wool carpet in a very dry room and touch a metal surface, you sometimes see "sparks." What are the "sparks"? _____
_____

Strategy Check

_____ Can you use friction to produce electrical charges?

_____ Can you demonstrate that opposite electrical charges attract, while similar charges repel?

| NAME | DATE | CLASS |

Chapter 2
LABORATORY MANUAL
Density and Buoyancy 8

Density is the mass per unit of volume. Buoyancy involves mass and volume. The buoyant force is the upward push exerted on an object by a liquid. When the mass of the displaced liquid is equal to the mass of the object, the object floats.

Strategy
You will determine the densities of fresh water, salt water, and an egg.
You will deduce the relationship between density and buoyancy.

Materials

balance	heat source	spoon
beakers (250 mL and 1000 mL heat proof)	measuring tray	stirring rod
egg	pan	water
graduated cylinder (50 mL)	salt	

Procedure
1. Measure 25 grams of salt into the measuring tray on the pan balance.
2. Heat 1 liter of water in the pan. Dissolve the salt in the water.
3. Pour the salt water into the liter beaker and let it cool to room temperature.
4. Determine the mass of 10 mL of the salt water. Record it in Table 8-1. Pour the salt water back into the beaker.
5. Determine the mass of 10 mL of water at room temperature. Record it in the table.
6. Determine the mass of the egg. Record it in the table.
7. Determine the volume of the egg. Record it in the table.
8. Carefully pour 250 mL of water on top of the cool salt water. Pour the water down the side of the beaker using the stirring rod. *Do not mix.*
9. Slip the egg into the beaker using the spoon. Observe and record its position.
10. Stir the solution, and observe what happens to the egg.

Data and Observations
Table 8-1

	Mass	Volume (cm³)	Density (g/cm³)
Water		10 cm³	
Salt water		10 cm³	
Egg			

Questions and Conclusions

1. Calculate the density of the water, salt water, and egg. Show your work. _____
   _____

   Record the densities in Table 8-1.

2. What happened to the egg when you added it to the separated water and salt water? _____
   _____

3. Compare the density of the egg to that of water and salt water. _____
   _____

4. What happened to the egg after you mixed the salt water and water together? _____
   _____
   _____

5. State the relationship between density and buoyancy. _____
   _____
   _____

6. Explain, in terms of density, why a person is able to float in water. _____
   _____
   _____

7. Is it easier for a person to float in seawater or in fresh water? _____
   _____
   _____
   _____

8. Explain how a balloon inflated with helium floats in air. _____
   _____
   _____

Strategy Check

____ Can you determine densities experimentally?

____ Can you state the relationship between density and buoyancy?

| NAME | DATE | CLASS |

Chapter 2
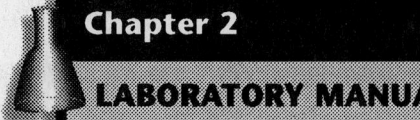
LABORATORY MANUAL
• States of Matter 9

Three common states of matter are solid, liquid, and gas. A fourth state of matter, the plasma state, exists only at extremely high temperatures. Differences among the physical states depend on the distance between the atoms or molecules and on the rate of movement of the atoms or molecules. Pressure and temperature control these two factors.

Strategy
You will observe the characteristics of a solid.
You will change a gas to a liquid.
You will compare the characteristics of a solid, a liquid, and a gas.

Materials
beaker (1000 mL)
ice cubes (frozen from 500 mL of water)
ice cube tray
plastic drinking glass (cold or add an ice cube)
water

Procedure
1. Mark the level of the top of the ice cubes while they are still in the tray. Remove the ice cubes and place them in the beaker. Record the characteristics of ice in Table 9-1.

2. Let the ice cubes melt. Record the volume and characteristics of the resulting water in Table 9-1.

3. Pour the water back into the tray. Mark the level of the top of the water on the tray. Under "Other characteristics" in Table 9-1, record whether this level is higher or lower than that of the ice.

4. Place the cold glass in a warm area. After a few minutes record your observations in Table 9-1.

5. Place an ice cube in the beaker of water. Observe whether or not it floats. Record your observations in Table 9-1.

Data and Observations

Table 9-1

Material	State of matter	Takes shape of container	Other characteristics
Ice cubes		Yes No	Floats Yes No
Water volume ___ mL			Higher/Lower in tray than ice
Glass	Observations: Beads of water appear on it.		
Beaker with ice	Observations: Floats		

Copyright © Glencoe/McGraw-Hill, a division of the McGraw-Hill Companies, Inc.

Questions and Conclusions

1. What is solid water called? _____ Liquid water? _____
   Water as a gas? _____

2. Did the ice cube sink or float in water? _____ Explain. _____
   _____

3. Which occupies more volume, an equal amount of water or ice? _____
   Explain. _____
   _____
   _____

4. Where did the water on the glass come from? _____
   What are the characteristics of water as a gas? _____
   _____
   _____

5. What change caused the water vapor to change to a liquid? _____
   _____

6. If you changed the water to water vapor in a pressure cooker, what volume would the water vapor occupy? _____

7. Compare the characteristics of water as a solid, a liquid, and a gas. _____
   _____
   _____
   _____

Strategy Check

_____ Can you observe the characteristics of a solid?

_____ Can you observe a gas change to a liquid?

_____ Can you compare the characteristics of a solid, a liquid, and a gas?

Chapter 3
LABORATORY MANUAL
Crystal Formation 10

Early in Earth's history, the crust was produced by the cooling of magma. When this molten rock flows into cracks, its temperature is about 1200°C. As the atoms of the different elements that make up the magma cool and slow down, they group themselves into a regular order to form a solid or crystal. This grouping is always the same for a given substance and is referred to as a mineral. When the magma cools to about 500°C, most of the minerals have crystallized out. The remaining minerals are dissolved in water. As the hot solution cools still more and finds its way to the surface where there is less pressure, the water evaporates and the rest of the minerals crystallize out. If the cooling is slow, large crystals result. If the cooling is fast, small crystals result. If the cooling is very fast, and the atoms do not have time to arrange themselves into regular order, an amorphous substance such as opal or glass results.

Strategy

You will observe crystal growth from a melt.
You will see mineral crystals in a sample of granite.
You will discover the effect that cooling rate has on crystal size.
You will discover processes that result in crystal growth.

Materials

beaker tongs
clear small medicine bottle with cap
dilute silver nitrate solution
eyedropper
fine copper wire
goggles
granite samples
hot plate
magnifying glass
microscope (optional)
microscope slides
salol

Procedure

Part A
1. Using the magnifying glass, look at the sample of granite. The granite was once molten. The minerals that make up the granite can be recognized by their different colors.

Data and Observations

Table 10-1

2. Fill in the data table below by placing an X in the appropriate box.

Mineral (color)	Having a definite shape	Shapeless
a) White or pink		
b) Black and shiny		
c) Black and dull		
d) Clear		

Questions
Part A

1. The clear material in granite is called quartz. It is nearly the last to crystallize out from a melt (500°C). Why do you suppose quartz is shapeless? _____

_____

2. Were the mineral crystals in granite easy to see with the unaided eye? _____

3. What can you say about the cooling rate of granite? _____

_____

Procedure
Part B

1. Place a clean fine copper wire (you may have to clean it with steel wool) about 1 cm long on a clean microscope slide.

2. Put the slide on the stage of a microscope or on a piece of white paper if you are using a hand lens.

3. From the dropper bottle marked silver nitrate solution, put 1 drop of the dilute silver nitrate on the copper wire and immediately watch what happens. **CAUTION:** *Do not spill the silver nitrate or get any of it on your clothes or hands.*

4. Draw a representative sample of the growth and the copper wire in the box below.

Questions
Part B

1. The pattern you have drawn is called a dendritic pattern and is made of silver. Is there a regular pattern to the growth? _____

2. Is the pattern repeated? _____

3. Are there plane surfaces that might suggest an orderly arrangement of atoms? _____

4. Look up the word "crystal" in your textbook. If this activity were to occur in nature, could the silver dendrite be called a crystal? Explain. _____
_____
_____

5. On a very cold day, the water vapor in the air of a warm room contacts the cold windowpane and freezes. The result is a feathery, almost dendritic pattern of ice. Would the dendritic pattern be the result of fast or slow crystallization? What is your evidence? _____
_____

Procedure
Part C
1. Place a few crystals of salol into a small glass bottle and screw on the lid.

2. Heat the bottle in a water bath. The salol melts at 43°C, which is a little above body temperature.

3. When the salol has melted, lift the bottle out of the water bath using beaker tongs. Pour some of the liquid salol onto a clean microscope slide.

4. Watch the crystal growth using a magnifying glass or microscope.

Questions
Part C
1. The salol melts at 43°C, but when placed in the closed bottle, it melts at a higher temperature. Why? _____
_____
_____

2. Where did the crystals begin to form in the "puddle" of salol? _____
_____

3. Where would you expect to find the irregular shaped crystals? _____
_____

Strategy Check

_____ Can you recognize different crystals in a rock sample?

_____ Can you list some natural processes that result in crystal formation?

_____ Can you associate crystal size with the rate of cooling?

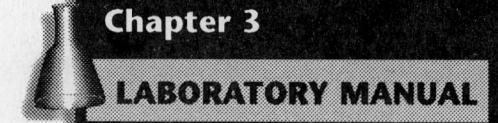

Chapter 3
LABORATORY MANUAL
Minerals and Optical Crystallography 11

One of the methods scientists use to identify mineral crystals is called optical crystallography. This involves the use of cross-polarized light. When white light passes through a polarizer, the light is composed of seven color waves traveling at different velocities but in the same direction. If the white light passes through a crystal, the atoms of the crystal may cause one of the color waves to break up or interfere with another color wave. Instead of seeing white light, an observer sees a colored light. This color is called an interference pattern. Every class of crystals produces its own color patterns. The interference color will vary with the thickness of the crystal and the direction in which the light travels through the crystal.

Strategy
The colors of the crystals will be more dramatic if the room is dark.
You will construct a simple crystal analyzer.
You will analyze a set of known crystals.
You will use your results to identify an unknown crystal.

Materials
crystal system table, p. 63,
   Glencoe Earth Science
flashlight
halite (clear)
mica, thin piece

pencils (colored)
polarizing film (2 pieces)
quartz (clear)
unknown crystal

Procedure
1. Place one piece of polarizing film on top of the flashlight.
2. Place a thin piece of mica on the film and cover the mica with the second piece of film.
3. Turn on the flashlight.
4. Rotate the top piece of film until colors are visible. Sketch the color pattern in Table 11-1.
5. Rotate further and see if different colors become visible.
6. Repeat for each sample including the unknown sample.
7. Refer to a table on crystal systems and record the system to which each known sample belongs.

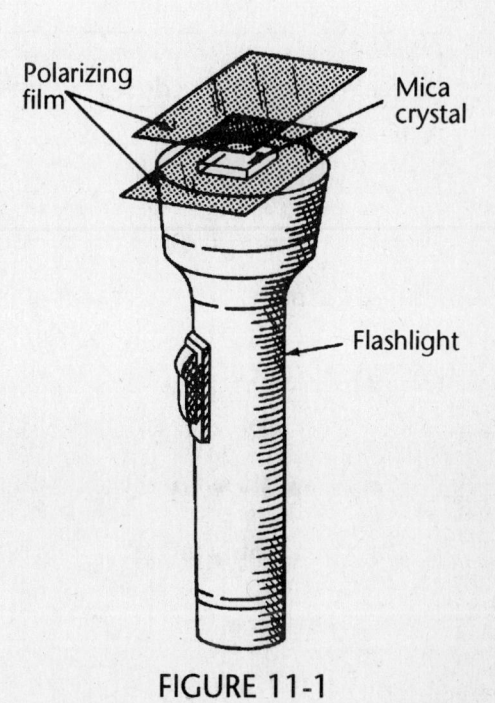

FIGURE 11-1

Data and Observations

Table 11-1

Crystal	Crystal system	Color patterns
Mica		
Quartz		
Halite		
Unknown		

Questions and Conclusions

1. Did you see different color patterns for each sample? _____

2. Explain why different color patterns for each sample are possible. _____
_____
_____

3. To what crystal system does your unknown sample belong? _____
   Defend your answer. _____
   _____
   _____

4. What is the name of your unknown sample? _____

Strategy Check

_____ Can you construct a simple crystal analyzer?

_____ Can you analyze crystals?

_____ Can you identify an unknown crystal?

| NAME | DATE | CLASS |

Chapter 3
LABORATORY MANUAL

Mineral Resources 12

All available mineral resources come from Earth's crust. These resources are called nonrenewable because they exist in finite or definite amounts. Mineral resources are an important part of our everyday life.

Strategy
You will survey a classroom in your school for metal resources.
You will survey a classroom in your school for nonmetal resources.

Materials
2 or 3 sheets of graph paper
pencils (colored—red, blue)
reference books on minerals

Procedure
1. Your teacher will assign you a classroom in your school to survey for metal and nonmetal resources. List all the items in the room that are made of metals and nonmetals in Table 12-1.
2. On graph paper, draw a scale floor plan of the classroom that you are surveying.
3. On your floor plan, draw a red dot each time you list a metal and draw a blue dot for each nonmetal.
4. List on the survey sheet the mineral or rock source of each item listed.

Data and Observations (See page 28.)

Questions and Conclusions
1. Does your classroom contain more metal items than nonmetal ones, or more nonmetal items than metal ones? _____

2. List the five most expensive metal items on your survey. _____

   Why are they more expensive than others? _____

3. What metals are used in the construction of your school? Nonmetals? _____

4. What mineral is used in making glass? _____

5. Are there electric lights or radiators in your school? _____ What metal is used in the wires? _____

Copyright © Glencoe/McGraw-Hill, a division of the McGraw-Hill Companies, Inc.

6. What fuel is used to heat your school? _____ Do you think this is a mineral fuel? _____ Explain. _____
_____
_____

7. Explain briefly why there is a drain on Earth's mineral resources. _____
_____
_____
_____

Data and Observations

Table 12-1

Item	Metal	Nonmetal	Mineral/Rock source

Strategy Check

____ Can you recognize metal mineral products?

____ Can you recognize nonmetal mineral products?

____ Can you understand the limitations of Earth's mineral resources?

Chapter 3
LABORATORY MANUAL
Removal of Waste Rock 13

If a substance is to be classified as an ore, it must be extracted, processed, and sold at a profit. The substance may be a single mineral or a group of minerals. Without profit, no one can continue in the mining business. In general, mining and treating ores yields only a small amount of the valuable mineral product compared to the large amounts of waste rock handled during the operation.

Waste rock is removed from ore by both physical and chemical processes. Sometimes the ore is crushed and the waste rock is picked out by hand. Usually, however, other processes are used. Magnetic minerals can be separated from waste rock by using large magnets. In some cases, such as panning for gold, the waste rock floats away. Some minerals are lighter than the waste rock. They can be recovered by allowing the unwanted rock to sink.

Strategy
You will use several of the methods industry employs to separate the wanted from the unwanted material.
You will remove iron by magnetism.
You will separate salt by filtering and distilling.
You will use gravity to separate minerals from waste rock.

Materials
bar magnet
beaker (500 mL)
2 beakers (250 mL)
corn syrup (white)
filter paper to fit funnel
flask (250 mL)
funnel (clear)
graduated cylinder (50 mL)
heat source
nails (iron)
pan
pepper
pie pans
salt
water

Procedure
1. Mix the sand and nails together in a pie pan. Write down two ways of separating them in Table 13-1.

2. Draw the bar magnet across the bottom of the pan. When the nails are assembled in one area, remove them by drawing the magnet over the surface of the sand.

3. Mix together approximately 125 mL salt and 50 mL pepper. Write down two methods of separating them in Table 13-1.

4. Stir the combination of salt and pepper into 250 mL of water. Pour the water through filter paper into the flask.

5. Allow the filter paper to dry. Observe and record your observations in Table 13-2.

6. Pour the liquid in the flask into the pan and boil the water off. Record what sediment remains in Table 13-2.

7. Place a clean filter in the funnel. Put the funnel in the flask and pour 50 mL of corn syrup into the funnel. Add a mixture of 2 or 3 nails and 15 mL sand.

8. Allow the funnel to stand for about 15 minutes. Diagram the position of the sand and nails in Table 13-2.

Data and Observations

Table 13-1

Ways to separate sand and nails:

1. _____
2. _____

Ways to separate salt and pepper:

1. _____
2. _____

Table 13-2

Filter paper observations: _____
_____
_____

Sediment remaining after water is boiled off: _____

Diagram funnel here.

Questions and Conclusions

1. Which separation depends on gravity? _____
   Explain. _____
   _____

2. Which method for separating iron from sand works better? _____
   _____

3. When you mix pepper and salt, do you form a compound or a mixture? _____

4. Is a mixture more like a rock or a mineral? Explain. _____
   _____

5. After you pour the salt, pepper, and water solution through the funnel, what does the filter paper look like? _____
   Explain. _____
   _____

6. Which of the processes that you used is the filtration method of separation? _____
   _____

7. Which process is the extraction method? _____

8. Which process is the evaporation method? _____

Strategy Check

_____ Can you separate salt from pepper? From water?

_____ Can you separate iron from sand by two different methods?

NAME _____ DATE _____ CLASS _____

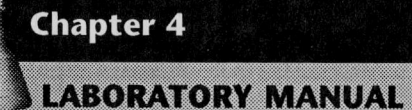

Chapter 4
LABORATORY MANUAL
Gas Production in Magma 14

Magma is a fluid solution of rock-forming materials and gases that eventually cools to form igneous rock. Some liquids and gases within the magma are less dense than the main mass. These gases, and some very hot liquids, rise to the top of the magma. They carry some early-forming crystals along with them as they rise.

Strategy
You will make "magma" that produces gas.
You will observe the effect of the gas on solids within the magma.
You will compare action in your activity with the probable action of gases within a magma.

Materials
baking soda
balance
2 beakers (500 mL)
6 mothballs
spoon or stirring rod
vinegar (white)
water

Procedure
1. Mix about 10 g of baking soda in 250 mL of water. Stir until the baking soda dissolves.
2. Place the mothballs in the beaker and allow them to settle to the bottom.
3. Add 125 mL vinegar to the beaker and stir vigorously.
4. Record your observations; be sure to touch the beaker.

Data and Observations
Observations: _____
_____
_____
_____
_____
_____
_____
_____

Copyright © Glencoe/McGraw-Hill, a division of The McGraw-Hill Companies, Inc.

31

Questions and Conclusions

1. Vinegar reacts with soda water to form carbon dioxide gas. Explain what happens to the mothballs.
   _____
   _____

2. Why do the mothballs eventually stop moving? _____
   _____

3. Why do less dense materials tend to collect at the top of the magma? _____
   _____

4. Olivine crystals form early in magma. How would you explain the presence of olivine crystals in a basaltic lava flow? _____
   _____
   _____

5. What might happen to the mothballs if a large volume of carbon dioxide gas is formed under pressure, and then the pressure is suddenly released? _____
   _____

6. How is this activity similar to the eruption of Mount St. Helens in Washington? _____
   _____
   _____
   _____

Strategy Check

_____ Can you produce gas in "magma"?

_____ Can you observe the effects of gas on solids within the magma?

_____ Can you compare your activity with the probable activity of gases within a magma?

NAME _____ DATE _____ CLASS _____

Chapter 4
LABORATORY MANUAL
● Metamorphic Processes 15

Metamorphic processes involve both temperature and pressure. Metamorphic processes are classified according to whether the effects are mainly caused by pressure or by heat. Whenever temperature rises, pressure also rises; whenever pressure rises, temperature rises. Metamorphism can occur at Earth's surface when hot lava bakes the rocks. However, most metamorphic changes occur underground.

Strategy
You will find a relationship between pressure and temperature.
You will observe the changes in clay caused by heating.

Materials
Part A
hand bicycle pump

Part B
balance
burner or another heat source
clay flowerpot (solid bottom)
clay shards
magnifying glass
piece of dry potter's clay

Procedure
Part A
1. Place your thumb over the end of the tubing of the pump.
2. Feel the lower and upper ends of the pump. Record your observations of the temperatures in Table 15-1.
3. Quickly pump the handle several times.
4. Feel both ends of the pump and record in Table 15-1.
5. Record what happens when you take your thumb off the tubing.

Part B
1. Trace the outline of the piece of potter's clay in Table 15-2.
2. Determine the mass of the clay.
3. Observe and record any other characteristics of the clay.
4. Place the piece of dried potter's clay on top of the broken pieces of clay in the flowerpot.
5. Heat the flowerpot strongly. **CAUTION:** *Be sure to keep hair and clothes away from an open flame.*
6. Allow the clay to cool. Determine the mass of the fired clay. Trace the outline of the clay again. Observe and record any other changes.

Data and Observations

Table 15-1

	Temperature of pump	
	Lower end	**Upper end**
Before pumping		
After pumping		

Table 15-2

Clay (Before heating)		Clay (After heating)	
Mass _____ (g) Other properties:	Outline:	Mass _____ (g) Other properties:	Outline:

Questions and Conclusions

1. In what part of the pump is the pressure greatest? _____

2. What happens to the air molecules in the pump when you press down on the handle? _____
   _____

3. What happens to molecules of air or water in deeply buried rocks? _____

4. Why does temperature increase when molecules are compressed? _____

5. How is this activity similar to the processes that occur underground? _____
   _____
   _____
   _____
   _____

Strategy Check

____ Can you determine the relationship between temperature and pressure?

____ Can you observe changes in clay caused by heating?

NAME _____ DATE _____ CLASS _____

Chapter 4

LABORATORY MANUAL • Concretions 16

Concretions are features found in sedimentary rocks. They may be spheres or flattened ovals. Concretions are formed when successive layers of cementing material are deposited and precipitated around a central core. Concretions may be harder than the surrounding rock. They are found as the surrounding rock is weathered.

Strategy
You will make a concretion.
You will observe the process of precipitation.
You will demonstrate the process by which some sedimentary rocks are formed.

Materials
cardboard (stiff)   patching plaster   spoon
dropper   pie pan (disposable)   water
food coloring   rock with flat side   waxed paper

Procedure
1. Place a piece of waxed paper on a piece of cardboard.

2. In the pie pan, mix some plaster with water. Add the water drop by drop until the plaster will spread but not run.

3. Place the stone flat side down on the waxed paper. Spread the plaster over its exposed sides. Record the color of the layer in Table 16-1.

4. Clean the pie pan thoroughly.

5. Place the stone in a location where it can dry undisturbed.

6. On the second day, repeat Steps 3 through 5. Mix a drop of food coloring in the plaster. Record the color of the layer in Table 16-1. Let dry.

7. On the third day, add another layer using a different color. Record in the table.

8. On the fourth day, add another layer using a third color. Record. Contours may be thicker in some places since concretions are not always smooth.

9. On the fifth day, remove the cardboard and waxed paper. Sketch the bottom of the concretion on page 36.

Data and Observations
Table 16-1

Day	Color	Day	Color
1		3	
2		4	

Sketch concretions here.

Questions and Conclusions

1. What do the different layers represent? _____
   _____

2. What causes the different layers in naturally formed concretions? _____
   _____

3. Why are concretions found only in sedimentary rocks? _____
   _____
   _____

Strategy Check

_____ Can you make a concretion?

_____ Can you observe the process of precipitation?

_____ Can you demonstrate how some sedimentary rocks are formed?

Chapter 5

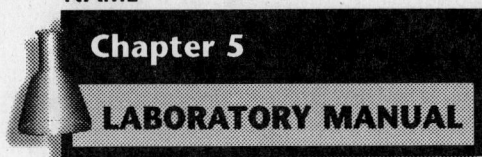

LABORATORY MANUAL

Determining Latitude 17

Ancient people used the stars to help them keep on course during journeys. In the early days of sailing ships, sailors also used the stars to help them steer a true course. The sailors used a simple instrument called a sextant and the North Star to determine their position. You can also determine your position in degrees of latitude using a simple sextant and the North Star.

Strategy
You will construct a simple sextant.
You will determine your approximate latitude in degrees.

Materials
cardboard, stiff
protractor, Figure 17-2
glue
scissors
map of the United States or world atlas
nut or metal washer
plastic straw
string, 20 cm
tape
thumbtack

Procedure
1. Cut out the protractor in Figure 17-2. Glue the protractor to a piece of cardboard.
2. Attach one end of the string to the nut.
3. Attach the free end of the string to the protractor's center hole, using the thumbtack.
4. Tape the plastic straw to the straight edge of the protractor. Your sextant should look like Figure 17-1.
5. On a clear night when the North Star is visible, sight the North Star through the straw.
6. Anchor the string to the sextant using your thumb or fingers. The degree marking on the sextant is the altitude of the North Star. This is your approximate latitude.
7. Record your latitude in Table 17-1.
8. Repeat steps 5, 6, and 7 three times.

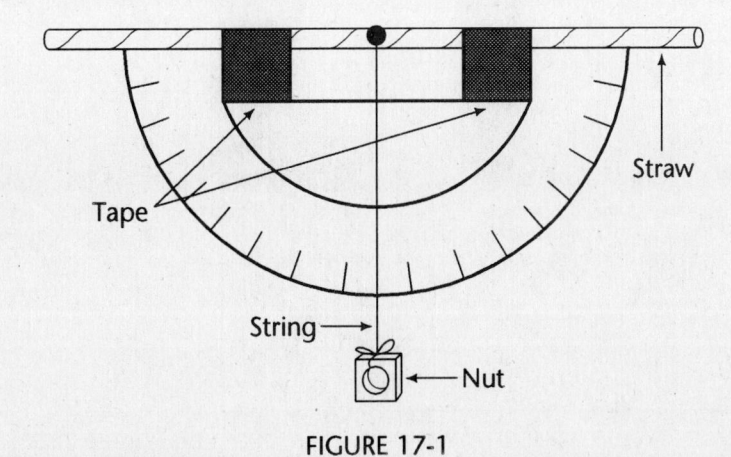

FIGURE 17-1

Data and Observations

Table 17-1

	Latitude (°)
Trial 1	
Trial 2	
Trial 3	
Average	

Questions and Conclusions

1. Calculate the average latitude of your three trials. Show your work. _____

2. How does your observed latitude compare to the latitude given in the atlas for your location? _____

3. Explain any differences between your observed latitude and the latitude listed in the atlas.
_____

4. What was the purpose of having three trials and finding an average? _____

Strategy Check

____ Can you construct a simple sextant?

____ Can you determine your approximate latitude?

FIGURE 17-2

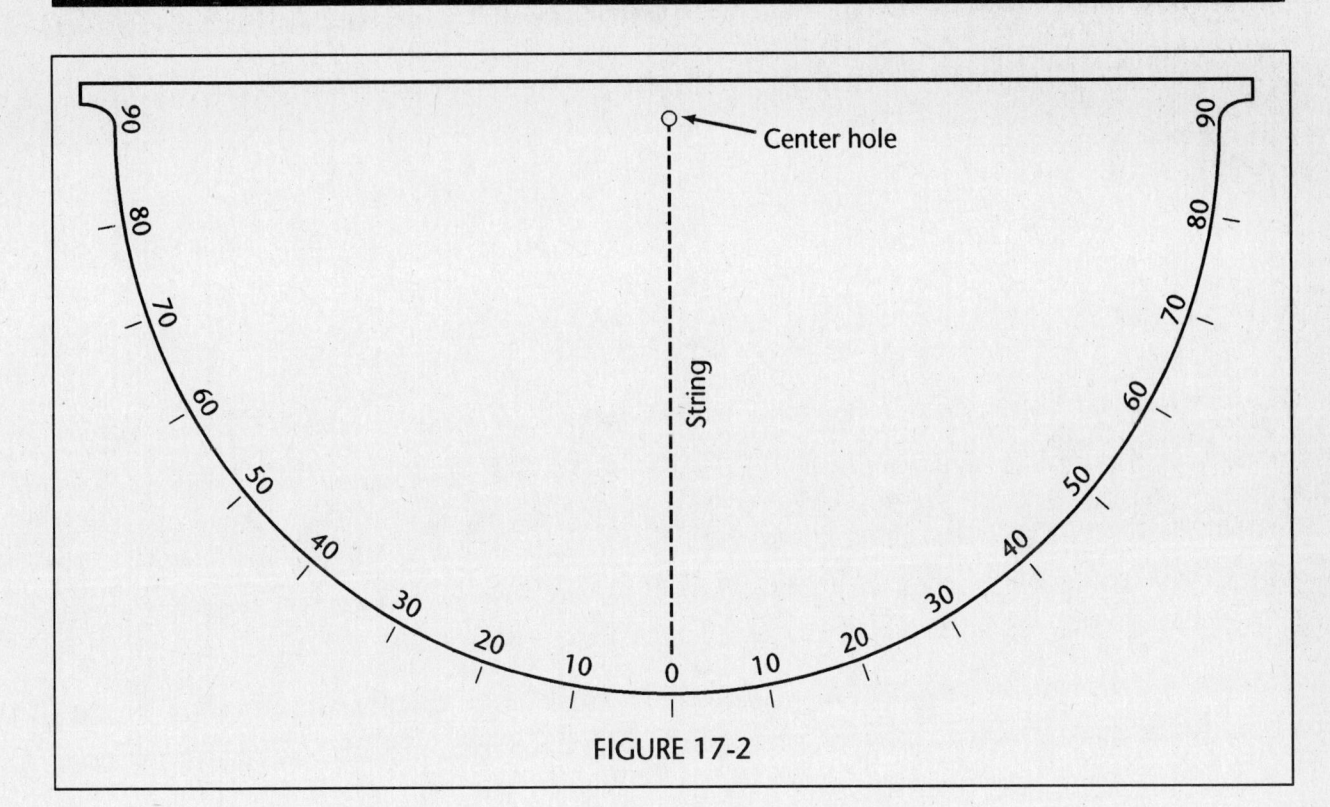

Chapter 5
LABORATORY MANUAL
Time Zones 18

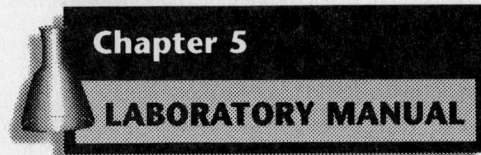

Time zones around Earth are bounded by imaginary lines called meridians of longitude, or meridians. Meridians are used to indicate locations east or west of the Prime Meridian (0° longitude), which passes through Greenwich, England. On the opposite side of Earth (180° longitude), the international date line is used to adjust time zones. Earth's surface is divided into 24 units, with 15° longitude to each unit. Each of the 24 units represents a time zone with 1 hour of difference between meridians. At the international date line, a day is lost going west or gained going east.

Strategy
You will plan a trip that will take you across several time zones.
You will use distance, speed, and time zones to determine local arrival time.
You will use the international date line to determine arrival date.

Materials
meterstick
world map showing longitude and time zones

Procedure
1. You will fly west from Washington, DC, to Wake Island in the Pacific Ocean. You will leave Washington, DC, at 8 A.M., Monday, January 1.
2. Locate Washington, DC, on the world map. Record its longitude in Table 18-1.
3. Locate Wake Island and record its longitude.
4. Measure the map distance between Washington, DC, and Wake Island in centimeters. Record this measurement and the map scale in Table 18-1.
5. Record the number of time zones you cross.

Data and Observations
Table 18-1

Washington, DC _____	(longitude)
Wake Island _____	(longitude)
Map scale _____	
Map distance between Washington, DC, and Wake Island _____	
Number of time zones crossed _____	

Questions and Conclusions

1. What is the distance, in kilometers, from Washington, DC, to Wake Island? _____
   Show your work. _____
   _____

2. Your plane travels at a speed of 1127 km/h. Calculate the number of hours you will be flying.
   _____
   _____

3. Calculate the local time and date of your arrival at Wake Island. _____
   _____

4. How many degrees of longitude did you cover in your flight? _____

5. Did the sun set during your flight? Explain. _____
   _____
   _____

6. If you did not change your watch as you passed through each time zone, what time would your watch read when you arrived at Wake Island? _____

7. Why are time zones necessary? _____
   _____
   _____

8. What is the purpose of the international date line? _____
   _____
   _____

Strategy Check

_____ Can you explain why time zones are necessary?

_____ Can you explain why the international date line is necessary?

_____ Can you use time zones to determine local time in other parts of the world?

NAME _____ DATE _____ CLASS _____

Chapter 5

LABORATORY MANUAL • **Comparing Maps 19**

A globe is the best model or picture of Earth because it is shaped like Earth itself. However, a globe would be rather difficult to fit into your pocket. Geographers have designed several different flat models of Earth. These flat models, called maps, can be folded or printed in the book.

Strategy
You will compare some map projections.
You will observe disadvantages of each type of map.
You will consider the probable best use of each type of map.

Materials
globe Homolosine map, Figure 19-2 4 sheets tracing paper
graph paper (metric) Mercator map, Figure 19-1

Procedure
1. Record the scales of the globe and your maps in Table 19-1.

2. Using the tracing paper, trace the outlines of Greenland, North America, and South America from the globe and Figures 19-1 and 19-2. Include Greenland in your tracing of North America.

3. Place the globe tracings of Greenland, North America, and South America over metric graph paper. Determine their areas in cm² by counting the number of square centimeters contained in each tracing. Count only squares that are totally or more than half contained within the boundaries of the tracings.

4. Determine the areas of Greenland, North America, and South America in square kilometers by performing the following calculation. . . .
    Globe or map area in cm² multiplied by the scale of the map squared equals the area on Earth in cm². This value is then divided by 10 000 000 000 (1×10^{10}), to obtain the area in km². (There are 10 000 000 000 or 1×10^{10} cm² in one km².) Record the areas in Table 19-1.

5. Using the procedures in steps 3 and 4, determine the areas of Greenland, North America, and South America in square kilometers on the Mercator and homolosine maps and record these areas in Table 19-1.

6. Compare the latitude and longitude lines on the map with these lines on the globe. Record your observations in Table 19-2.

Data and Observations
Table 19-1

Landmass	Area (km²)		
	Globe	Mercator map	Homolosine map
Greenland			
North America			
South America			
Scale			

Table 19-2

Model	Latitude	Longitude
Globe		
Mercator map		
Homolosine map		

Questions and Conclusions

1. Why does Greenland appear so large on the Mercator map? _____
_____
_____

2. How do Greenland and South America actually compare in size on the globe? _____
_____

3. Which of the two maps represents more correctly the sizes of Greenland and South America?
_____

4. Which of the two maps is a truer model of Earth's landmasses? _____

5. What happens to the longitude circles on a Mercator map? _____
   What happens to latitude lines on a Mercator map? _____

6. What happens to the latitude lines on a homolosine map? _____

7. Why would a Mercator map be more useful than a homolosine map to an airplane pilot?
_____
_____

8. If you were asked to map the route you follow to school, would you make a Mercator map or a homolosine map? _____ Why? _____
_____

Strategy Check

____ Can you compare maps?

____ Can you see disadvantages of each map?

____ Can you determine the best probable use of each type of map?

NAME _____ DATE _____ CLASS _____

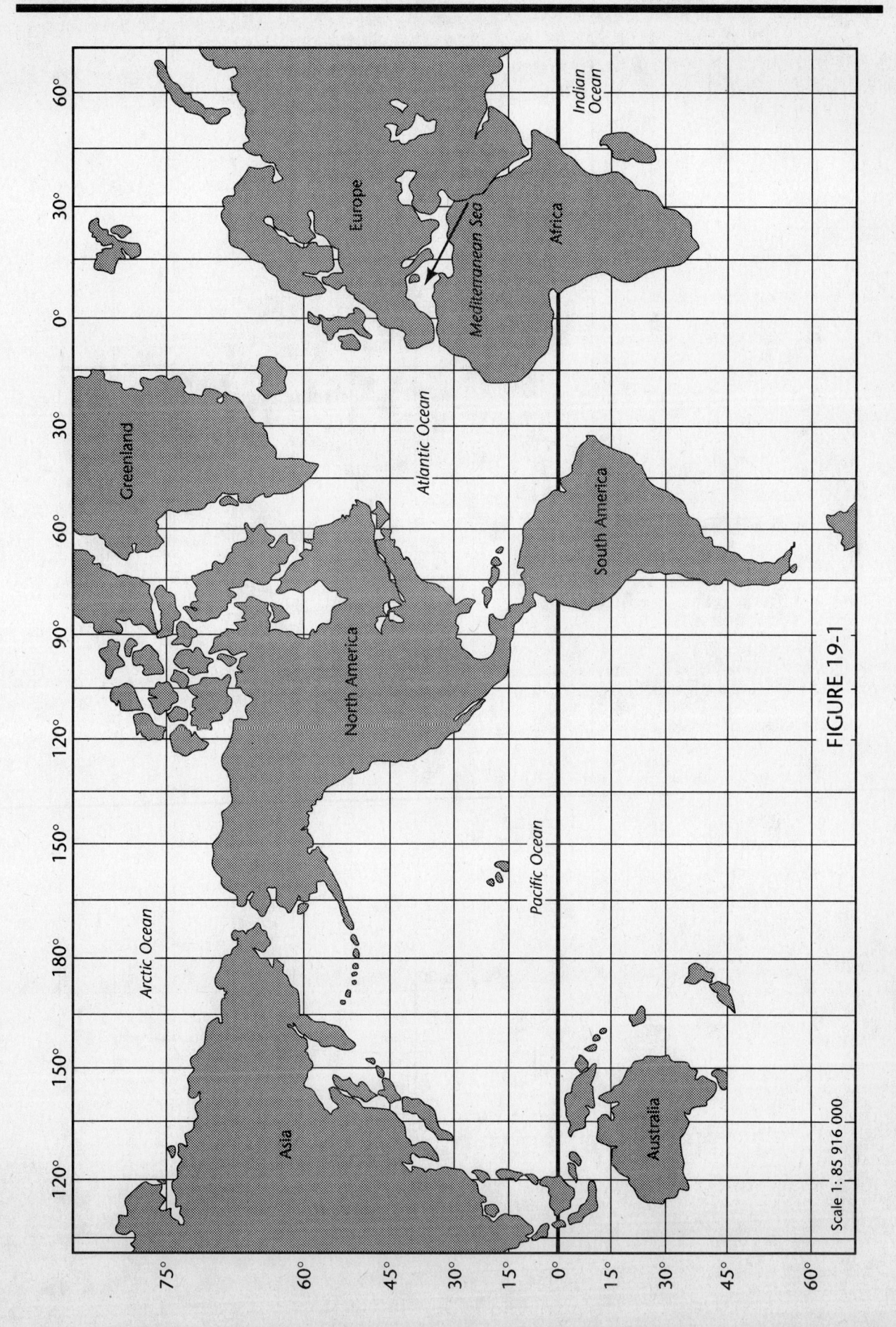

FIGURE 19-1

Scale 1: 85 916 000

FIGURE 19-2

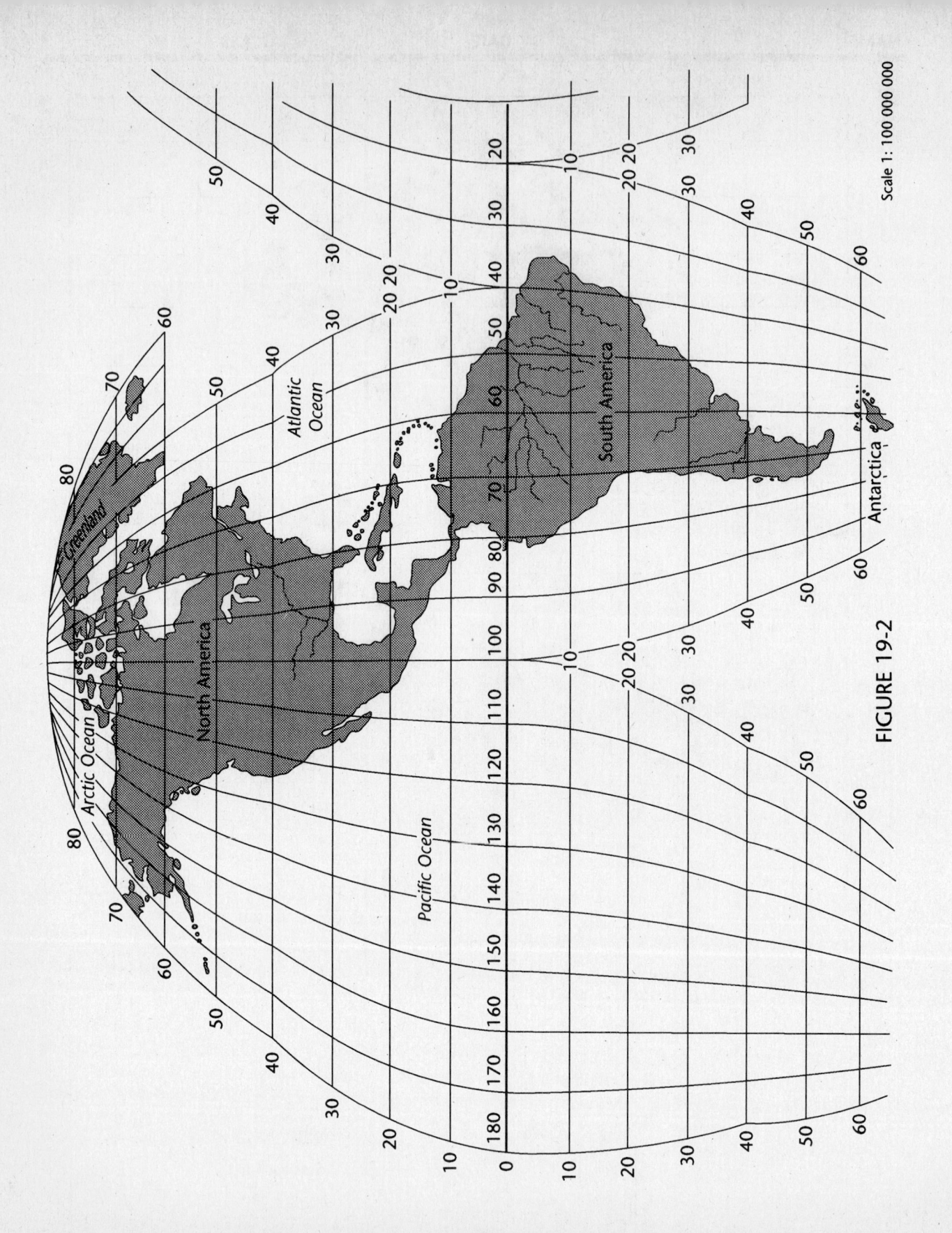

Scale 1: 100 000 000

NAME   DATE   CLASS

Chapter 5
LABORATORY MANUAL
Using a Clinometer 20

Layered beds are the best clues to structural changes. Originally, most sedimentary rocks were deposited in approximately horizontal layers. The amount of change from the horizontal position indicates the amount of twisting, or diastrophism, that the sedimentary rocks have undergone. For field work, a clinometer is used to measure the amount of dip, or tilt, of layered beds. Dip is the angle between a horizontal plane and the tilted bedding plane or top of the layer. The amount of dip is always expressed in degrees and is written beside the dip symbol: ⋏ 35°.

Strategy
You will construct a clinometer.
You will use the clinometer to measure the dip angle.

Materials
books (several)
cardboard (stiff)
drill
glue or paste
paper rivet
scissors
string, 10 cm
washer (heavy)

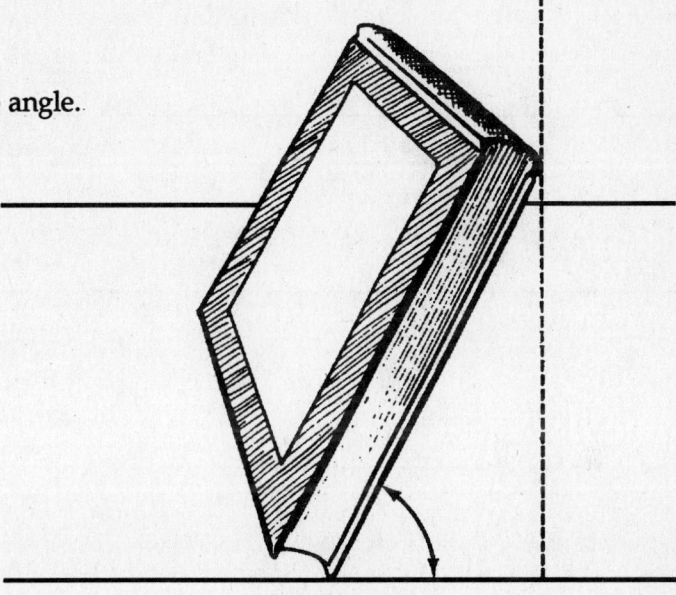

FIGURE 20-1

Procedure
1. Cut out the clinometer box, Figure 20-2. Cut along the solid lines.
2. Glue the pattern to an equal-sized piece of stiff cardboard.
3. Drill a small hole in the center of the cardboard.
4. Tie the string securely around the paper rivet, push the rivet through the hole, and open the prongs of the rivet.
5. Tie the washer to the other end of the string.
6. Test the clinometer by placing it upright on the edge of a flat desk. The string should hang over the zero degrees position.
7. Tilt one book and support it with a second book. Measure the dip angle. Draw a diagram of the "rocks" and label the dip angle.
8. Repeat Step 7 for several different tilts.

Data and Observations

Table 20-1

Rock diagram	Dip angle

Questions and Conclusions

1. In what direction must you place your clinometer on a layer of rock to determine the dip?
   _____

2. If a bed is vertical, how many degrees of dip does it have? _____

3.. If a bed is horizontal, what is the dip angle? _____

4. Strike is a horizontal line drawn on the surface of an outcropping layer indicating the compass direction in which the outcrop lies. At what angle to the strike of a bed do you place your clinometer to get the maximum dip angle?

Strategy Check

_____ Can you construct a clinometer?

_____ Can you measure dip angles using a clinometer?

FIGURE 20-2

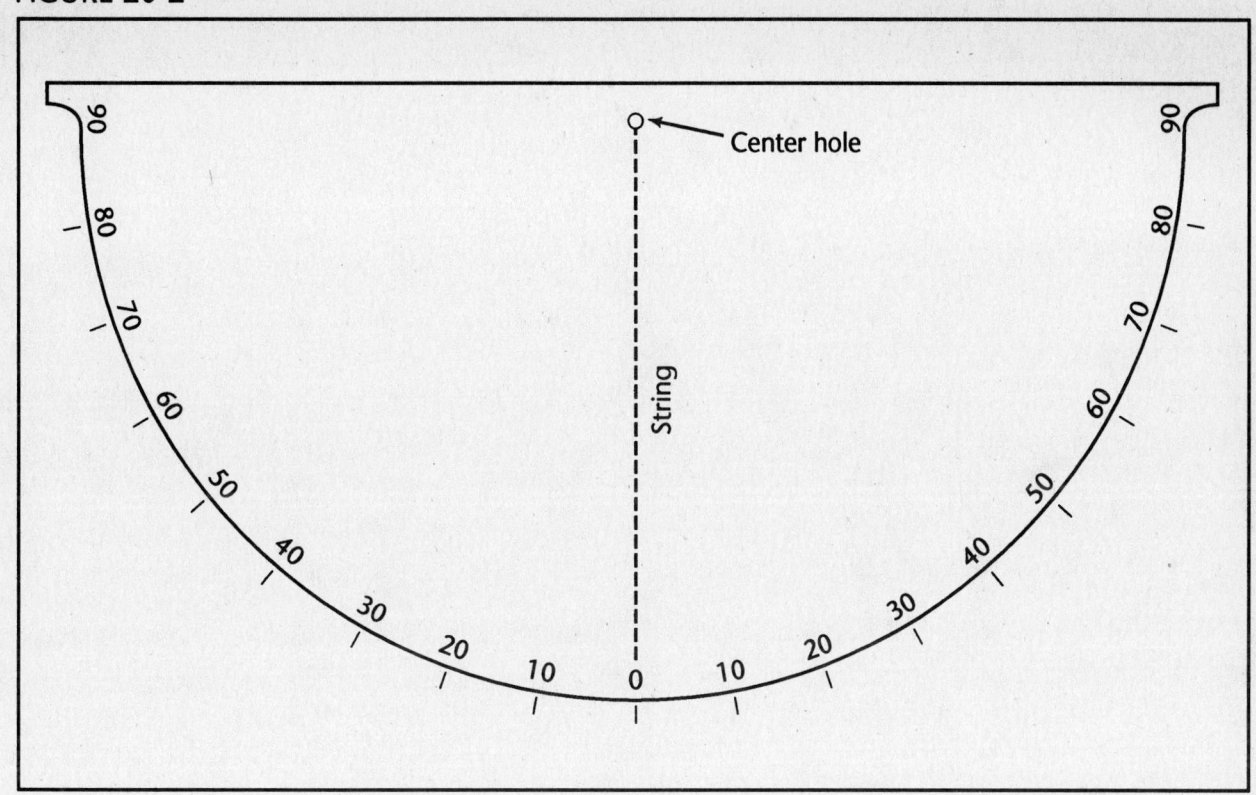

| NAME | DATE | CLASS |

Chapter 6
LABORATORY MANUAL
Chemical Weathering 21

Rocks are mixtures of minerals that are either elements or chemical compounds. Chemical weathering is the chemical reaction of these minerals with carbon dioxide, water, oxygen, or other substances at Earth's surface. For example, in minerals containing iron, the iron reacts with oxygen in the air to form rust. Rotted plant material combines with water to form humic acids that cause chemical weathering.

Strategy
You will cause a chemical reaction between a copper strip and combined salt and vinegar at room temperature.
You will observe a chemical reaction between iron and atmospheric oxygen.

Materials
apron
beaker (100 mL)
copper strip (dirty)
goggles
graduated cylinder
iron(II) sulfate, $FeSO_4$
pie pan (disposable)
salt
test tube
vinegar (white)
water

Procedure

1. For the first activity, place a copper strip in the pie pan and place 5 mL salt on the strip.

2. Carefully pour 30 mL of vinegar over the copper. Record your observations in Table 21-1.

3. Wash the salt and vinegar off the copper. **CAUTION:** *The material formed is an acid. Avoid contact with skin and clothing.*

4. For a separate activity, mix 5 g of iron(II) sulfate in 50 mL of water. **CAUTION:** *Iron(II) sulfate is poisonous. Avoid contact with skin.* Record the color of the solution and any other observations in Table 21-1.

5. Let the beaker and the copper both stand undisturbed overnight.

6. Next day, observe the beaker and the copper. Record your observations in Table 21-1.

Data and Observations
Table 21-1

	Start	Next day
Copper strip		
Beaker $FeSO_4$		

Questions and Conclusions

1. What happened to the copper when you poured the vinegar over the salt? _____
_____

2. Is cleaning copper a chemical or physical process? _____

3. Explain what happens to the clean copper left in the air overnight. _____
_____
_____

4. Why does this reaction follow the cleaning of the copper? _____
_____
_____

5. Explain what you observe in the beaker of $FeSO_4$. _____
_____
_____

6. Is this a chemical or physical change? _____

7. Explain the rust-colored stains you see on some rocks. _____
_____
_____

8. How might a soil layer protect bedrock from chemical weathering? _____
_____
_____
_____

Strategy Check

____ Can you observe chemical reactions at Earth's surface?

____ Can you demonstrate that chemical reactions can occur at room temperature?

| NAME | DATE | CLASS |

Chapter 6
LABORATORY MANUAL
Soil Infiltration by Groundwater 22

Whether rainwater enters the soil or runs off the surface depends on a number of factors. One of the most important of these factors is the type of soil. The rate at which rainwater enters the soil determines whether or not flooding occurs. It also determines whether or not septic tanks can be installed safely in a given region. If liquid from the tanks flows outward faster than the soil can absorb it, no filtering action occurs, and sewage reaches the surface and contaminates the area.

This laboratory activity is one of the tests that engineers use to decide whether or not septic tanks are acceptable for a given area. Engineers make the test directly in the ground, sinking the can as far as possible. You may make the test in the same way, or you may construct a simulated soil sequence and do your testing in the classroom.

Strategy
You will measure the rate at which water filters through the soil.
You will plot the rate of infiltration against time.
You will compare various materials to see which are most suitable for filtering groundwater.

Materials
beaker (500 mL)
can opener
cardboard (thin)
cheesecloth, 30 cm x 30 cm
slab clay
dishpan or sink
graph paper
500 mL gravel
juice can, large
metric ruler
pen (felt-tip)
2 pencils
plastic bucket
pointed stick, 30 cm long
500 mL sand (fine)
scissors
500 mL soil
tape (masking)
watch with second hand
water

Procedure
1. With the can opener, cut out both ends of the can. Place the cheesecloth across the bottom of the can and fasten it with tape.

2. Place the can in the dishpan, cloth side down. Raise the can slightly by resting it on the two pencils.

3. In this experiment, do not fill the can more than about half full. Place a layer of gravel in the bottom of the can. Place a layer of clay on the layer of gravel. Place a layer of sand on top of the clay. Place a thick layer of soil on top of the sand.

4. Make a cardboard cover for the can. Cut a small hole (about the diameter of the pointed stick) in the cardboard cover. Also, cut a small portion from one side of the cover. Through this hole, you will be able to observe the water level.

5. Fill the rest of the can with water. Place the cover over the top of the can.

6. After about one minute, insert the pointed stick into the can through the small hole until it just touches the top of the water. With the felt-tip pen, draw a line on the stick where it intersects the cardboard cover of the can.

7. Mark the water depth on the stick every 60 seconds until the water touches the soil. Determine the various water depths by measuring from the point of the stick to the first mark, second mark, and so on. Record all your data in Table 22-1.

Copyright © Glencoe/McGraw-Hill, a division of the McGraw-Hill Companies, Inc.

53

Data and Observations

Table 22-1

Time (min)	Water depth (cm)	Time (min)	Water depth (cm)

Graph your data using the vertical axis for Depth of water (cm) and the horizontal axis for Time (min).

Questions and Conclusions

1. Is the rate of infiltration constant? _____ Explain. _____

2. Would the rate of infiltration be faster in wet soil or in dry soil? _____ Why?

3. Which layer infiltrates most slowly? Explain how you got your answer. _____

4. Which layer is most likely to allow the water to move through it too rapidly to be a good filter? Explain how you could design an experiment to find out. _____

Strategy Check

____ Can you measure the rate at which water filters through soil?

____ Can you make a graph that shows the rate of infiltration?

____ Can you compare various materials to see which is suitable for filtering groundwater?

NAME _____ DATE _____ CLASS _____

Chapter 7
LABORATORY MANUAL

• Mass Movements 23

The force of gravity causes loose material to move downslope. Sometimes water helps to move the material. Water makes the material heavier and more slippery.

Downslope movements of earth materials may be sudden or slow. Landslides and mudflows are sudden movements. Rocky slopes tend to move as landslides; clay and sand materials may become mudflows.

Creep is an example of slow earth movement. Even when a slope is covered by vegetation, the soil may creep to a lower level.

Strategy
You will cause mass movements.
You will classify the mass movements.

Materials
1 L clay
1 L gravel
meterstick
plastic bucket
protractor
1 L sand
sprinkling can
stream table with hose
water
4 wood blocks

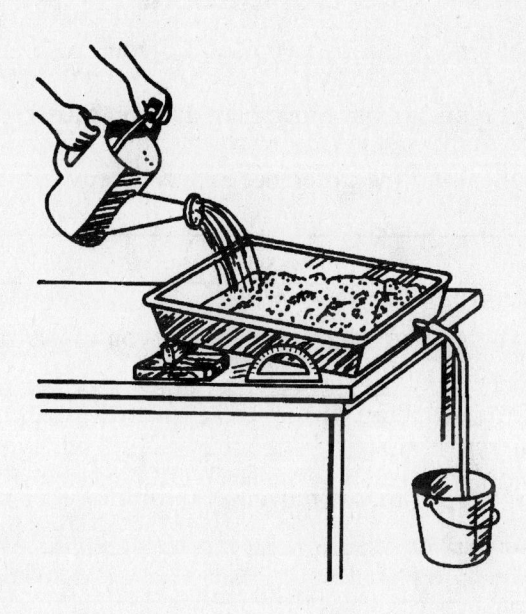

Procedure
1. Set up the stream table as shown in Figure 23-1.
2. Place the protractor with its flat edge down on the table that is supporting the stream table. Position the protractor next to the lower end of the stream table. Use the protractor to measure the slope angle of the stream table. Record the angle in Table 23-1.
3. Place the clay in the upper end of the stream table.
4. Pour the sand over the clay. Wet the sand and clay thoroughly until it moves.
5. Observe and record in Table 23-1 how the mass moves.
6. Add two more blocks under the stream table. Measure and record the new slope angle of the stream table.
7. Move the sand and clay back to the upper end of the stream table.
8. Pour water over the sand and clay until it moves. Record how the mass moves.
9. Remove the sand and clay. Spread a thin layer of clay in the upper end of the table.
10. Spread gravel over the clay. Pour water over the clay and gravel and observe the motion. Record your observations.

Copyright © Glencoe/McGraw-Hill, a division of The McGraw-Hill Companies, Inc.

Data and Observations

Table 23-1

Material	Slope angle (°)	Speed of movement
Sand, clay		
Sand, clay		
Clay, gravel		

Questions and Conclusions

1. What type of mass movement did you cause in Step 3? _____

2. What type of mass movement did you cause in Step 7? _____

3. What caused the difference in speed between these two mass movements? _____
_____
_____

4. What type of mass movement did you cause in Step 9? _____
_____
_____

5. Which type of mass movement would occur during an extended period of heavy rain on a filled area? Explain. _____
_____
_____
_____

6. Which type of mass movement, creep or mudflow, is most destructive? _____
   Defend your answer. _____
_____
_____
_____

7. In an area that receives abundant rainfall, how are steep slopes kept from moving downhill?
_____

Strategy Check

____ Can you cause mass movements?

____ Can you classify mass movements?

NAME _____ DATE _____ CLASS _____

Chapter 7

LABORATORY MANUAL • **Model Glacier 24**

Valley glaciers start in the mountains where snow collects and remains year after year. When accumulation exceeds melting and the snow mass is thick enough, gravity starts the glacier moving downslope. The glacier can take over a river valley as it moves toward a lower elevation. The glacier gouges and scrapes the surface beneath the ice and changes the landscape in many ways.

Greenland and Antarctica have the only continental glaciers at present. Alaska and Canada have numerous valley glaciers.

Strategy
You will construct a model of a valley glacier.
You will show the rugged features a valley glacier forms as it moves and melts.

Materials
cardboard base, 21.5 cm x 28 cm
4 colors of modeling clay
paper for labels
tape (clear)
toothpicks

Procedure
1. On the cardboard base, form a mountain from the darkest piece of clay.
2. Use white clay to show the position of a glacier on your mountain.
3. Show the erosional features of the glacier. Use little flags to label these features using the toothpicks and paper.
4. You might wish to use a thin layer of green clay to show where vegetation has begun to appear.
5. Be sure to model each of the following features: U-shaped valley, hanging valley, cirque, terminal moraine, horn, and outwash plain.
6. Draw a diagram of your model and label the features. Draw your diagram on page 58.

Data and Observations (See page 58.)

Questions and Conclusions
Write a summary explaining how valley glaciers form and move and how they change the landscape.

_____
_____
_____
_____
_____

Data and Observations
Draw glacier diagram here.

Strategy Check

____ Can you construct a model of a valley glacier?

____ Can you correctly model and label the features left by a valley glacier?

NAME	DATE	CLASS

Chapter 8
LABORATORY MANUAL
Transporting Soil Materials by Runoff 25

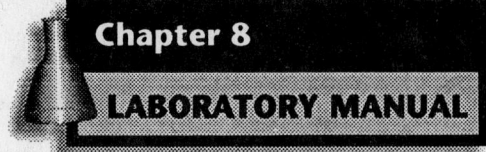

Some minerals present in the soil are dissolved and carried in solution by runoff. Other materials are picked up, or pushed along the ground surface, by runoff. Eventually, all of these materials are deposited.

Strategy
You will observe which of the soil components goes into solution.
You will determine which surface materials are carried a long distance and which ones are deposited nearby.

Materials
60 mL clay or mud
60 mL gravel
5 plastic drinking glasses (clear)
60 mL salt
60 mL sand (coarse and fine, mixed)
spoon
water

Procedure
1. Put 30 mL of clay into one glass, 30 mL of gravel into a glass, 30 mL of salt into a glass, and 30 mL of sand into a glass.
2. Take the leftover 30 mL of each material and put it into the fifth glass.
3. Add water to each glass and stir well. Record your observations in Table 25-1.
4. Observe the glasses three times during the next 30 minutes. Record your observations. On page 40, diagram the layers in the glass containing the mixture.

Data and Observations

Table 25-1 Observations during 30-minute period after stirring

	Beginning	1	2	3
Clay				
Sand				
Salt				
Gravel				
Mixture				

Sketch glass here.

Questions and Conclusions

1. What happens in each container? _____
_____
_____
_____

2. How are sandy materials and clay distributed in soil? Why are sediments sorted by size? _____
_____
_____
_____

3. What happens to the sand, salt, clay, and gravel carried by streams? _____
_____
_____
_____

4. In an arid climate where water is not penetrating the soil but is moving up to the surfaces of the soil from underground, where would you expect to find the soluble material? _____
_____
_____
_____

Strategy Check

____ Can you observe that some soil components go into solution?

____ Can you observe that some surface materials settle out of water more rapidly than others?

NAME _____ DATE _____ CLASS _____

Chapter 8
LABORATORY MANUAL • Capillary Action 26

During a rain, some of the water that moves downward toward the water table and zone of saturation is trapped in tiny, hairlike openings. These openings are called capillaries. Capillaries store molecules of water until a dry period. Then some of the water returns to the surface. Plant roots get moisture from "dry" soil as the moisture moves from saturated soil up the capillaries to the surface.

Strategy
You will demonstrate how moisture moves from saturated soil into the capillaries of dry soil.

Materials
beaker (500 mL)
celery stalk with leaves
food coloring (red)
pan
pencils (colored—green, red)
2 plastic drinking glasses (clear)
0.5 L sand (coarse)
scissors
water

Procedure
Part A
1. Fill the beaker half full of water and add a few drops of food coloring. Place the celery in the beaker. Draw a diagram of the celery showing the color of the celery under Data and Observations, Part A.

2. Observe and diagram the celery after two days under Data and Observations, Part A.

Part B
1. Remove the bottoms from the plastic glasses. Be careful not to crack the glasses.

2. Set the glasses upright in the pan. Fill each glass with sand.

3. Carefully pour water into one glass until the sand is saturated and some water flows into the pan.

4. Observe and diagram what happens to the water. Draw your diagram under Data and Observations, Part B.

Data and Observations
Part A

Beginning

After 2 days

Part B

Diagram pan here.

Questions and Conclusions

1. What happens in the glass of dry sand when the water reaches it? _____
_____
_____

2. Compare the action of the water in the sand to the action in the celery. _____
_____
_____
_____

3. How do you know capillary action occurs in the celery? _____
_____
_____

4. How could capillary action occur in the desert? _____
_____
_____
_____

5. What kind of rock would be best suited for capillary action? _____
_____
_____

6. Would it be good to dig up the soil around plants during a very dry period? _____
   Explain. _____
_____
_____

Strategy Check

_____ Can you demonstrate capillary action in celery?

_____ Can you demonstrate capillary action in soil?

Chapter 8
LABORATORY MANUAL
Carbon Dioxide and Limestone 27

When carbon dioxide is dissolved in water, it forms a weak acid. This acid dissolves limestone. Many caves have deposits of limestone (calcite) in the form of stalactites and stalagmites. Calcite is also found as the cementing material in many sandstones and other limestones. Thus, limestone can be dissolved beneath the surface and it can also be deposited beneath the surface.

Strategy
You will examine conditions under which carbon dioxide may be lost from a carbonated soft drink.
You will observe the effect of loss of carbon dioxide on the precipitation of calcium carbonate.
You will compare these processes to the natural processes.

Materials
apron
beaker (100 mL)
3 cans of carbonated soft drinks
goggles
hammer
ice cubes
limewater (Ca(OH)$_2$ solution)
nail
pan
plastic straw (flexible)

Procedure
1. Place one can of carbonated drink in the pan of ice cubes and allow it to cool.
2. When the can is cool, shake it and one of the other cans gently.
3. Remove the top from each of the two cans while holding the cans over the pan or the sink. Record what occurs in Table 27-1.
4. With the nail and hammer, make a small hole in the top of the third can. The hole should have about the same diameter as the straw.
5. Carefully slip the straw into the can. Hold the other end in the beaker filled with limewater. **CAUTION:** *Limewater may irritate the skin. Avoid contact.* Record your observations in Table 27-1.

Data and Observations
Table 27-1

Can	Observations
On ice	
Warm	
Limewater	

Questions and Conclusions

1. What gas is present in a carbonated drink? _____

2. What happened when you removed the tops from two of the cans? _____
   Why? _____
   _____

3. Which soft drink lost its carbon dioxide faster? _____ Why? _____
   _____
   _____

4. Describe what happens when the soft drink and the limewater are combined. _____
   _____
   _____

5. As the carbonic acid seeps through the roof of a cave, part of the water evaporates. What happens to the calcium carbonate? _____
   _____

6. If underground water circulates close to the vent of a volcano, it might dissolve carbon dioxide. Would increased pressure or high temperature cause the carbon dioxide to dissolve? _____
   _____
   _____

Strategy Check

_____ Can you determine the conditions under which carbon dioxide escapes from a soft drink?

_____ Can you observe the effect of the loss of carbon dioxide on the precipitation of calcium carbonate?

_____ Can you compare the processes observed here with natural processes?

NAME _____ DATE _____ CLASS _____

Chapter 8
LABORATORY MANUAL
Waves, Currents, and Coastal Features 28

Most of the waves that you see along the seashore are the result of wind blowing over the open ocean. In the open ocean, the waves don't seem to bother anything. As the waves move along the shoreline, however, they have a big effect on the land—transporting sediments from one place to another. Waves, tides, and currents are the reasons that shorelines constantly change.

Strategy
You will construct a simple wave tank.
You will observe some of the coastal features that form as waves interact with sloping sandy shorelines, underwater obstacles, and other topographic landforms.
You will study how waves form currents near the shore and how waves and currents transport sand along a shoreline.

Materials
clay, rocks, wood or rubber stopper (to simulate shoreline features)
grease pencil
sand (coarse and fine, clean)
talcum powder
wood block (15 cm x 3 cm x 7 cm) to use as wave generator
wood frame (1 m x 1 m x 10 cm) with plastic sheet for lining of wave tank

Procedure
1. Make a beach at one end of the wave tank. See Simulation A.

2. Using the grease pencil, make two marks 10 cm apart on the edge of the wave tank. See Simulation A.

3. Fill the wave tank with water to a depth of 3 cm.

4. Hold the wooden block in the water so that it is just touching the bottom of the wave tank and is parallel with the mark that is farthest away from the shore. Move the block toward the shore until it is parallel with the second mark. Lift the block out of the water. This entire motion should take about 1 second. Repeat the motion until you can produce uniform waves.

5. Once you are satisfied that you can produce uniform waves, set up the other simulations as illustrated in the diagrams. Each simulation will take at least 5 minutes. During that period of time, watch the waves and the movement of sand particles.

6. For each simulation, mark on the diagrams the crests of the waves as they approach the shore. Also indicate with the letter "e" where erosion is taking place and the letter "d" where deposition is taking place. Use arrows to indicate the direction of sand movement.

7. After you have finished the simulations, answer the questions on the following pages.

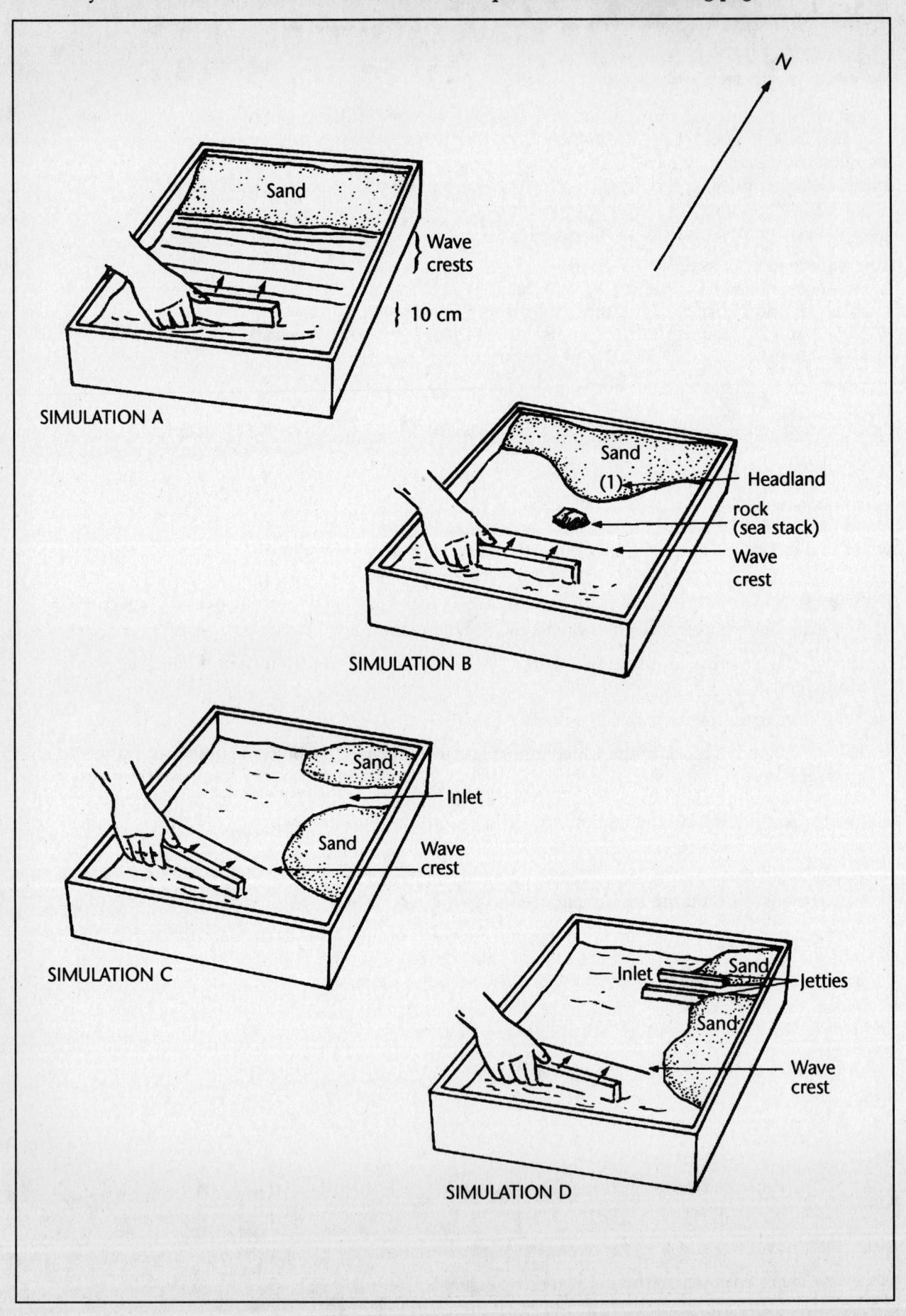

N

SIMULATION A
- Sand
- Wave crests
- 10 cm

SIMULATION B
- Sand (1)
- Headland
- rock (sea stack)
- Wave crest

SIMULATION C
- Sand
- Inlet
- Sand
- Wave crest

SIMULATION D
- Inlet
- Sand
- Jetties
- Sand
- Wave crest

NAME _____ DATE _____ CLASS _____

Questions and Conclusions

Simulation A

1. Describe the motion of the fine sand particles. _____
_____
_____

2. Predict what would happen if you continued the wave action for several days. _____
_____

3. If you were able to increase (winter condition) or decrease (summer condition) the energy of the waves, what changes would you see in the character of the beach? _____
_____
_____

4. Are the waves produced in simulation A deep or shallow water waves? _____

Simulation B

5. The island (sea stack) is the end result of the headland eroding. Describe the movement of sand in the area behind the sea stack. _____
_____

6. What topographic feature could be formed between the sea stack and the headland? ____

Simulation C

7. What happened to the beach? _____

8. What happened to the inlet? _____

9. What topographic feature could be forming at the mouth of the inlet? _____

10. Place some talcum powder in the water near the shore and watch its movement. This movement reflects the longshore current that you generated by changing the angle of the block (wave generator). If the longshore current continued for a long period of time, what would eventually happen to the inlet? _____

Simulation D

11. What effect did the wood jetties have on the deposition of sand? _____
_____

12. Why are jetties built on either side of an inlet? _____
_____

13. What would happen if the jetties were shortened? _____
_____
_____

Strategy Check

____ Can you identify coastal features formed by the deposition and erosion of sand by waves?

____ Can you identify how waves move materials along a shoreline, and how longshore currents develop?

NAME _____ DATE _____ CLASS _____

Chapter 9
LABORATORY MANUAL • Earthquakes 29

Earthquakes are frightening and often dangerous tremblings of Earth. Seismologists, scientists who study earthquakes, note that certain areas are earthquake-prone and likely to have damaging disturbances of Earth's crust. The risk of such disturbances in these areas is great because they lie over active geologic faults. Maps that pinpoint earthquakes all over the world show that the world's greatest seismic belt borders the Pacific Ocean. Every state in the United States, however, has had at least one earthquake of varying destructiveness. Seismologists believe that most earthquakes indicate active faults. Thus, once an earthquake has occurred, another may be possible.

Strategy
You will make a seismic-risk map of the United States.
You will study the occurrence of earthquakes in the United States.
You will determine which areas are earthquake-prone.

Materials
pencils (colored)

Procedure
1. Choose a color to represent each of the risk zones in the legend of the map on page 71.
2. Color the squares of the map legend to match the color chosen for each zone.
3. Plot the data from Table 29-1 on the map. Place one dot in the state for each recorded earthquake. Place two dots in the state for each high intensity earthquake.
4. Since California has such a large number of earthquakes, simply write the number of earthquakes on the state. In parentheses, write the number of high intensity earthquakes.
5. Color each state according to the legend. Example: California will be colored for Zone 3.

Data and Observations (See page 70.)

Questions and Conclusions
1. In what states have damaging earthquakes occurred? _____
_____
_____

2. In what region have damaging earthquakes been concentrated? _____
_____
_____
_____

3. What does a concentration of damaging earthquakes indicate about the underlying rock structure of the area? _____
_____
_____

Copyright © Glencoe/McGraw-Hill, a division of the McGraw-Hill Companies, Inc.

4. Based on this map, in which states might future earthquakes occur? _____
_____

5. In which state is earthquake risk highest? _____

Earthquake Locations

Table 29-1

State	Damaging earthquakes recorded	State	Damaging earthquakes recorded
Alabama	2	Montana	10 (3 high intensity)
Alaska	12 (2 high intensity)	Nebraska	3
Arizona	4	Nevada	12 (3 high intensity)
Arkansas	3	New Hampshire	0
California	over 150 (8 high intensity)	New Jersey	2 (1 high intensity)
Colorado	1	New Mexico	5
Connecticut	2	New York	5 (1 high intensity)
Delaware	0	North Carolina	2
Florida	1	North Dakota	0
Georgia	2	Ohio	6 (1 high intensity)
Hawaii	12 (2 high intensity)	Oklahoma	2
Idaho	4	Oregon	1
Illinois	10	Pennsylvania	1
Indiana	3	Rhode Island	0
Iowa	0	South Carolina	6 (1 high intensity)
Kansas	2	South Dakota	1
Kentucky	5	Tennessee	7
Louisiana	1	Texas	3 (1 high intensity)
Maine	4	Utah	9 (2 high intensity)
Maryland	0	Vermont	0
Massachusetts	4 (1 high intensity)	Virginia	5
Michigan	1	Washington	11 (2 high intensity)
Minnesota	0	West Virginia	1
Mississippi	1	Wisconsin	1
Missouri	9 (2 high intensity)	Wyoming	3

NAME _____ DATE _____ CLASS _____

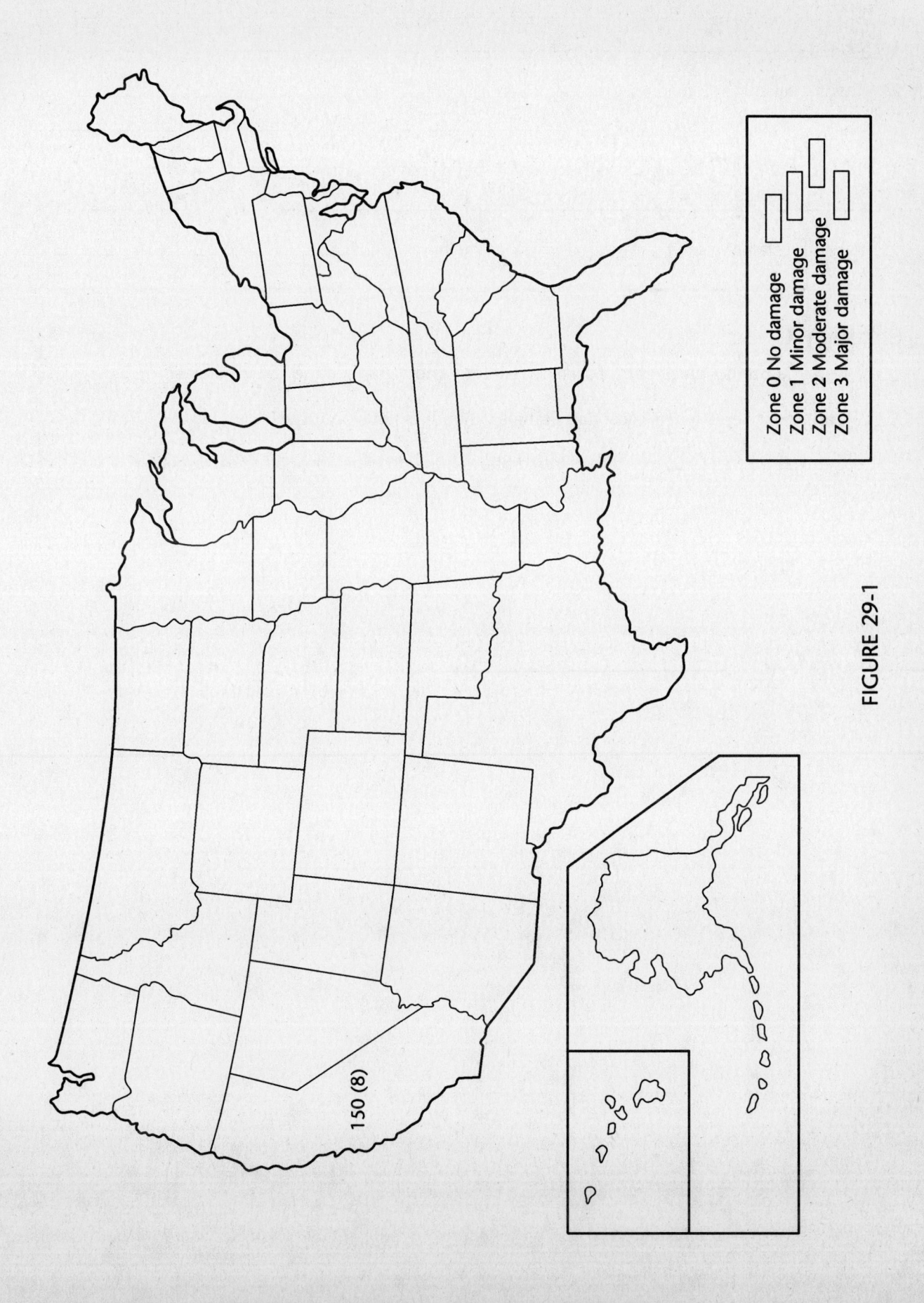

Zone 0 No damage
Zone 1 Minor damage
Zone 2 Moderate damage
Zone 3 Major damage

150 (8)

FIGURE 29-1

Copyright © Glencoe/McGraw-Hill, a division of the McGraw-Hill Companies, Inc.

71

6. Can you be sure that an earthquake could not occur in any area? _____
   Why? _____
   _____

7. Why is a seismic risk map useful? _____
   _____

8. Why do you think three states in the northern plains have had no damage from earthquakes?
   _____

9. Name two states where the earthquake risk is the least. _____
   _____

Strategy Check

_____ Can you predict the degree of seismic risk for various parts of the United States?

_____ Can you observe where most damaging earthquakes have occurred?

_____ Can you predict the parts of the United States likely to experience other earthquakes?

| NAME | DATE | CLASS |

Chapter 9
LABORATORY MANUAL
• Locating an Earthquake 30

When an earthquake occurs, the shock sends outward vibrations in all directions. Both minor and major shocks are recorded by instruments called seismographs. When reports from at least three stations conducting earthquake watches are compared, the location of the epicenter can be determined. The epicenter is the point on Earth's surface directly above the focus, the actual rock break that caused the earthquake.

The first vibration wave to reach the seismograph is called the P or primary wave. P-waves travel like sound waves, alternately compressing and expanding the rocks through which they pass. A second wave, the S-wave, takes twice as long to reach the station as the P-wave. S-waves are shear waves that shake the rocks in a manner similar to the way a bow vibrates violin strings.

Strategy
You will compute the distance of five different seismograph stations from a strong earthquake. You will use information from five seismograph stations to compute the location of the epicenter of an earthquake.

Materials
compass (drawing)
metric ruler

Procedure

1. Using the P-wave arrival times, compute the distance of each station from the earthquake center. The P-wave travels at a speed of 6 kilometers per second. Record the distances in Table 30-1.

2. On the map, Figure 30-1, draw an arc from each station using the computed distance as the radius of the circle. The map scale is 2 cm = 650 km.

3. Locate the epicenter of the earthquake. It is the point at which all arcs intersect (cross).

4. To check the accuracy of your epicenter determination, compute the arrival times of the S-waves. The S-wave travels at one-half the speed of the P-wave. Record in Table 30-1.

5. Check your distance computations using the S-wave arrival times.

Data and Observations
Table 30-1

Station	P-wave arrival time	Distance from epicenter using P-wave	S-wave arrival time	Distance from epicenter using S-wave
Rockville, MD	3 min, 20 sec			
Newport, WA	7 min, 55 sec			
Tucson, AZ	5 min, 50 sec			
Rapid City, SD	3 min, 45 sec			
McMinnville, TN	1 min, 15 sec			

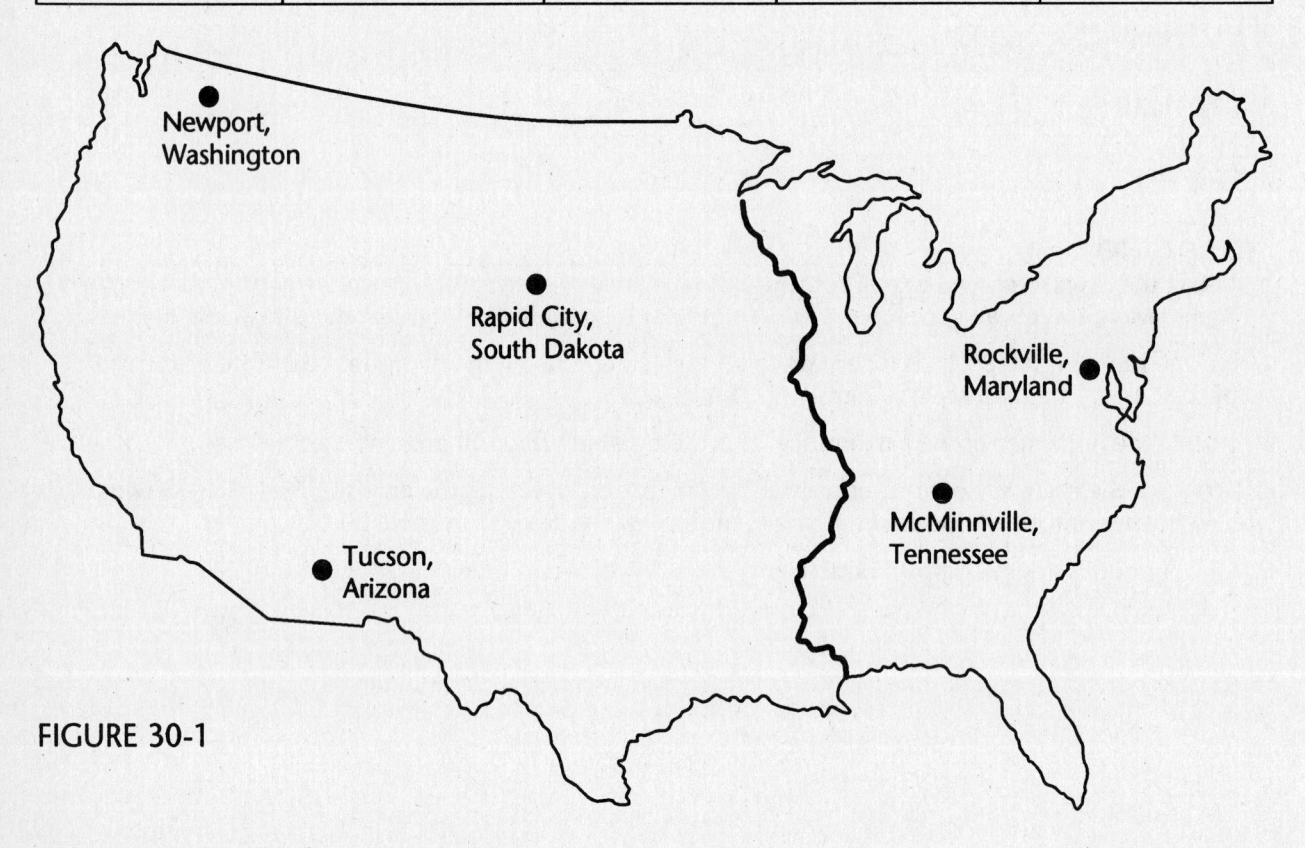

FIGURE 30-1

Questions and Conclusions

1. Where is the epicenter of an earthquake? _____

2. Do your figures for the S-wave agree with the distances computed from the P-wave arrival time?
_____

3. Near what city did the earthquake occur? _____

Using earthquake-wave arrival times for many earthquakes, scientists have plotted travel-time curves. Travel-time curves are line graphs that show how long it takes for a type of earthquake wave to travel a certain distance. Use the travel-time curve below to answer the following questions.

Earthquake Travel Time

Table 30-2

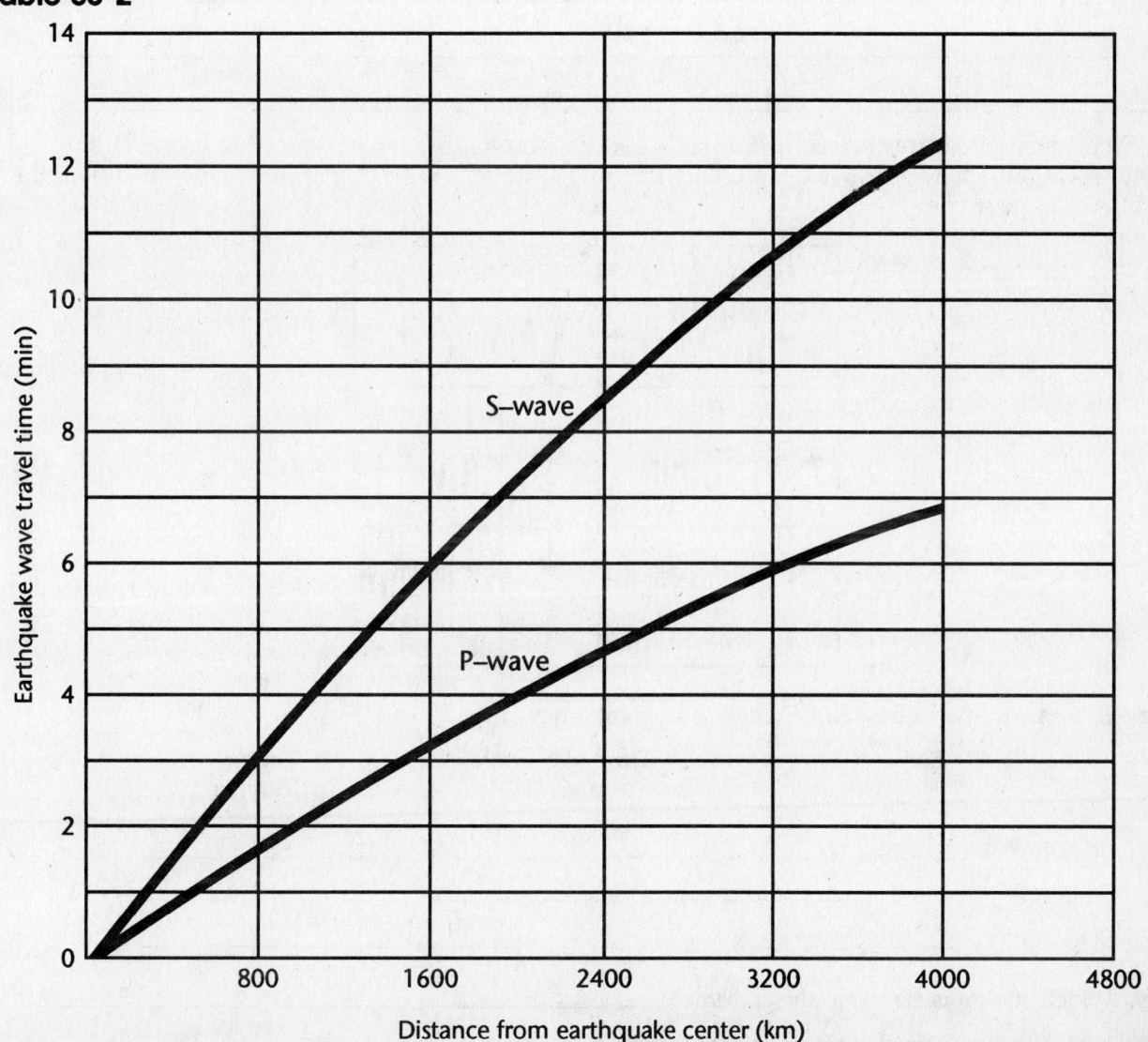

4. If a seismograph were located 1600 kilometers from the earthquake's focus, how long would it take the P-wave to travel this distance? _____

5. How long would it take the S-wave to travel 1600 kilometers? _____

6. How long would it be after the seismograph recorded the arrival of the P-wave before the seismograph recorded the arrival of the S-wave? _____

7. An earthquake was recorded at three different stations, A, B, and C. Use the travel-time curve to determine the distance from each station to the earthquake epicenter.

Station	Time between P- and S-wave arrival (min)	Distance to epicenter (km)
A	2.3	
B	2.8	
C	3.0	

Sections of seismograms, records traced by a seismograph, from three stations, A, B, and C, are shown below. Each vertical line represents 1 minute of time. Use the diagram to help you answer the following questions.

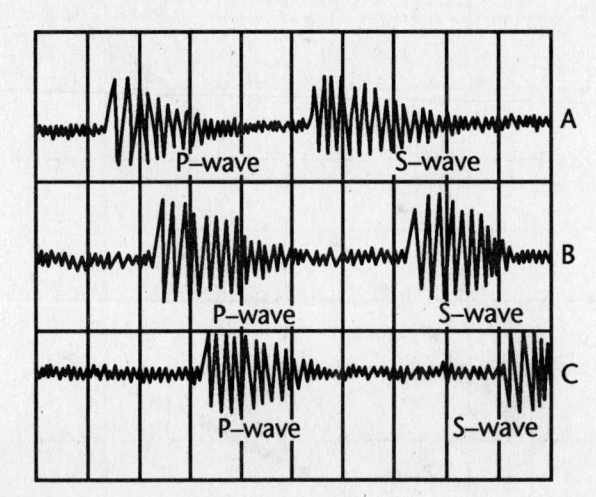

FIGURE 30-2

8. Estimate to the nearest half-minute the arrival times of the P- and S-waves at each station.

	Time of P-wave arrival	Time of S-wave arrival	Time difference
Station A			
Station B			
Station C			

9. Which station is closest to the epicenter? _____

Which station is farthest from the epicenter? _____

Strategy Check

_____ Can you compute the number of kilometers from each station to the epicenter using P-wave arrival times?

_____ Can you pinpoint the epicenter of the earthquake using your computed distances and the resulting arcs?

_____ Can you check your computations using S-wave arrival times?

| NAME | DATE | CLASS |

Chapter 10
LABORATORY MANUAL
Effect of Magma on Surrounding Rock 31

Magma sometimes seems to rise through solid rock. But as magma works its way upward through regions of solid rock called country rock, that rock actually melts to become part of the magma. As the rising liquid surrounds the country rock, the formerly solid rock softens, is separated from the surrounding rock, and is engulfed by the magma. Gases trapped in the magma tend to expand as the magma rises. This may crack the country rock, allowing the magma to rise further.

Strategy
You will demonstrate how an acid (vinegar) may penetrate shell without breaking it.
You will compare this process to the invasion of solid rock by magma.

Materials
balance
beaker (500 mL)
egg
meterstick
string, 30 cm
vinegar (white)
water

Procedure
1. Determine the mass and circumference of the egg. Record in Table 31-1.
2. Record characteristics such as color, hardness of shell, and smoothness of shell.
3. Place the egg in the beaker and cover with vinegar.
4. Allow the beaker to stand undisturbed overnight.
5. Pour off the vinegar and replace with water.
6. Allow the beaker to stand undisturbed for 3 days.
7. Pour off the water and examine the egg. Record its mass and circumference and any other changes.

Data and Observations
Table 31-1

Properties	Egg (before)	Egg (after)
Mass (g)		
Circumference (cm)		
Color		
Hardness of shell		
Other		

Questions and Conclusions

1. Compare the egg before and after soaking it in vinegar. _____

2. Why did you soak the egg in vinegar? _____

3. Explain, in order, the processes that caused the changes in the egg. _____

4. Use the processes you listed above and explain how magma changes the country rock it invades.

Strategy Check

_____ Can you demonstrate how vinegar is able to penetrate an egg?

_____ Can you compare this process to the actual invasion of rock by magma?

Chapter 10
LABORATORY MANUAL
Volcanic Preservation 32

On May 18, 1980, Mount St. Helens in Washington erupted for the first time in 123 years. Volcanologists, people who study volcanoes, estimated that Mount St. Helens spewed enough rock and ash to cover an area 2.6 kilometers square to a depth of 172.8 meters. This amount of ash is almost as much as Mt. Vesuvius poured onto Pompeii in A.D. 79. Organisms rapidly buried by the ash from volcanic eruptions may be preserved as fossils. Many examples were found in the excavation of Pompeii.

Strategy
You will form a "fossil" by drying.
You will compare the fossil to a living sample.

Materials
brush (soft)
cake tin with lid
flowers (several different kinds)
pencils (colored)
silica powder or borax

Procedure
1. Draw each flower specimen and record its properties in Table 32-1.
2. Pour silica powder into the tin to a depth of 5 centimeters.
3. Arrange fresh flowers on the silica powder. Carefully sprinkle silica powder over the flowers to a depth of 5 to 8 cm.
4. Put the lid on the tin and allow the tin to stand undisturbed for three weeks.
5. Carefully pour off the silica powder and examine the flowers.
6. Compare the appearance of the dried flowers to that of the fresh specimens.

Data and Observations
Table 32-1

Property	Fresh	Dried
Color		
Size		
Other		

Questions and Conclusions

1. How does the appearance of the dried flowers compare to that of the fresh flowers? _____
_____
_____

2. What was the purpose in using silica powder? _____
_____
_____

3. How is silica powder like volcanic ash? _____
_____
_____

4. What other natural agent might preserve fossils in the same way as volcanic ash? _____
_____
_____

5. Is your dried flower a true fossil? What else would have to happen to it? _____
_____
_____

Strategy Check

____ Can you form a "fossil" by drying?

____ Can you compare this fossil to a living sample?

NAME _____ DATE _____ CLASS _____

Chapter 11

LABORATORY MANUAL • **Continental Drift 33**

According to the theory of plate tectonics, the continents once formed one landmass named Pangaea. As new crust was formed at the mid-Atlantic rift, the seafloor began to spread apart. According to this theory, the seafloor spreading widened the Atlantic Ocean and separated Pangaea into the continents as we know them today.

Strategy
You will reconstruct a model of Pangaea.

Materials
2 pieces cardboard (thin)
maps, Figure 33-1
glue or paste
scissors
tape (clear)

Procedure
1. Cut out page 83 and glue it on the cardboard.
2. Cut out the continents.
3. Try to fit the continents into one large landmass.
4. When you have the best fit, tape the pieces to another piece of cardboard. Sketch your version of Pangaea.

Questions and Conclusions
1. Which two continents have the best fit? _____
_____

2. For the best arrangement, which continent forms the core of Pangaea? _____

3. Which continent is now part of Eurasia but, according to theory, was originally a separate continent that moved northward into its present position? _____

4. Why isn't the fit perfect if the continents were once part of Pangaea? _____
_____
_____

5. If the continents were drawn on a Mercator map, would your chances of finding a fit have been improved? Explain. _____
_____
_____
_____

6. Scientists theorize that the continents are still drifting apart. What will be the eventual position of North America with respect to Eurasia? _____

_____

_____

7. How did the Atlantic Ocean form? _____

_____

_____

_____

8. If the continents were once connected, what might be similar about the coastlines where they were connected? _____

_____

_____

Strategy Check

____ Can you make the continents fit together into one large continent?

____ Can you see how at one time the continents may have formed a super-continent called Pangaea?

FIGURE 33-1

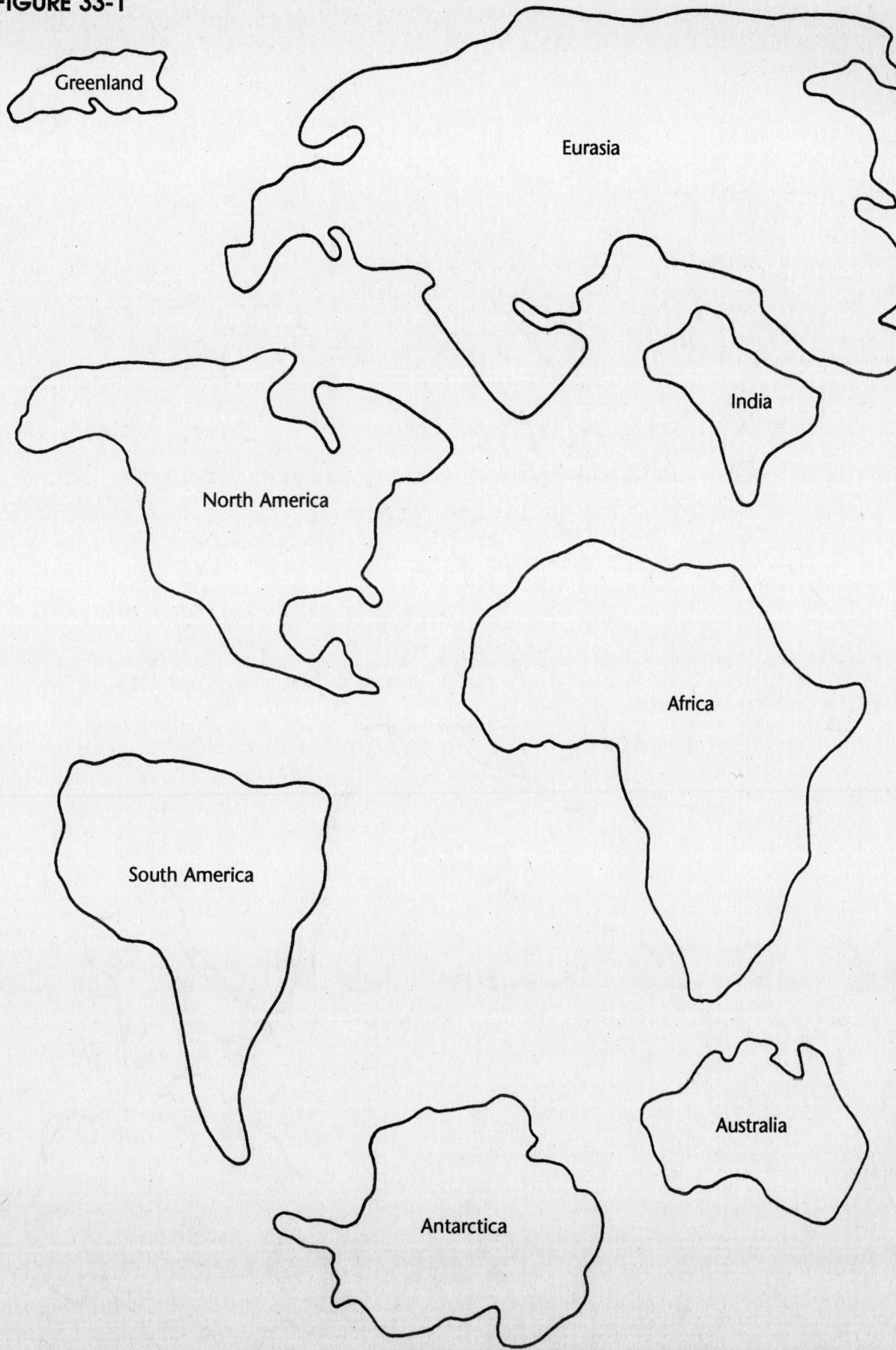

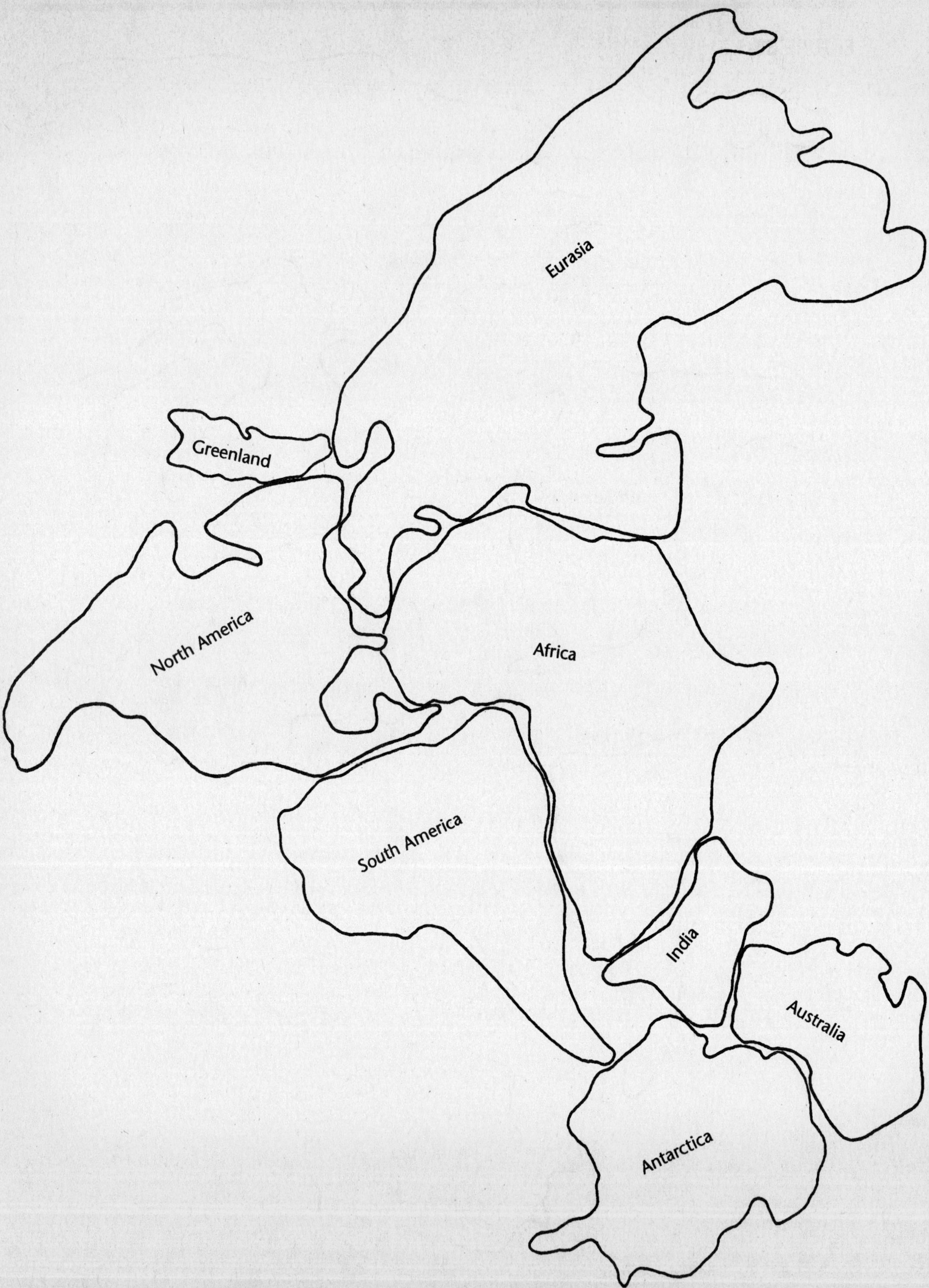
Eurasia
Greenland
North America
Africa
South America
India
Australia
Antarctica

NAME　　　　　　　　　　　　　DATE　　　　　　　　　　　CLASS

Chapter 12
LABORATORY MANUAL
Principle of Superposition 34

The principle of superposition states that beds in a series are laid down with the oldest at the bottom and successively younger layers on top. Beds may be exposed at the surface as a result of folding and uplifting or because of faulting. If part, or all, of a layer is removed by erosion and this surface is covered by a new deposit, the contact is called an unconformity. In some areas, river erosion will cut deeply enough to expose a number of layers, such as in the Grand Canyon.

Strategy
You will construct a map legend.
You will construct a block diagram of an area.
You will write the geologic history of the area.

Materials
block diagram, Figure 34-1
cardboard, thin
glue or paste
pencils (colored)
scissors
tape (clear)

Procedure
1. Set up a legend for your block diagram and select a color for each layer. Record the legend in Table 34-1.
2. Glue Figure 34-1 on the cardboard. Color the map according to your legend.
3. Cut out, fold, and tape the block diagram as instructed on Figure 34-1.

Data and Observations
Table 34-1

	Color
Layer A	
Layer B	
Layer C	
Layer D	

Questions and Conclusions

1. Which layer is oldest? _____ Explain. _____
   _____
   _____

2. What kind of structure do the layers have? _____
   _____
   _____

3. Why is the glacial till not folded? _____
   _____
   _____

4. What does the presence of the peat and soil layer in the glacial till tell you? _____
   _____
   _____
   _____

5. Was this a mountainous area prior to glaciation? _____ Explain. _____
   _____
   _____

6. How many advances of the ice occurred here? _____

7. Write the geologic history of the area illustrated in the block diagram. _____
   _____
   _____
   _____
   _____
   _____

Strategy Check

____ Can you set up a map legend?

____ Can you construct a block diagram?

____ Can you write the geologic history of the area illustrated by a block diagram?

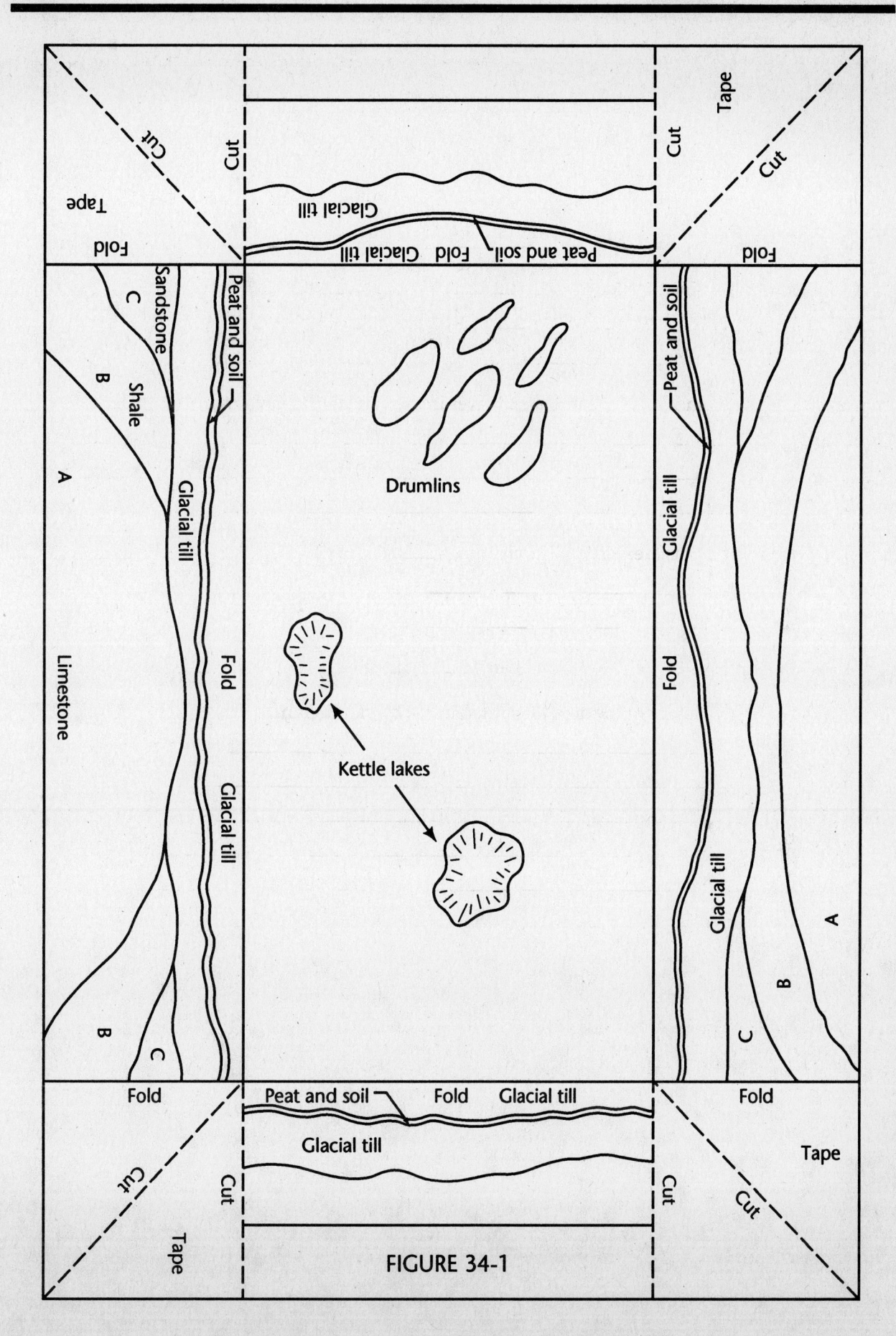

FIGURE 34-1

NAME _____ DATE _____ CLASS _____

Chapter 12
LABORATORY MANUAL • Carbon Impressions 35

Carbon impressions are a fairly common type of fossil, especially in forest areas. A leaf or soft-bodied animal is buried in soft mud. When the plant or animal decays, nothing is left but the carbon that was in the plant or animal. This carbon shows as a fineline impression of the plant or animal.

Strategy
You will make a carbon impression of a fern frond.

Materials
candle
fern frond
goggles
match
2 paper towels
petroleum jelly
plastic wrap
tweezers
2 sheets typing paper

Procedure
1. Spread a thin layer of petroleum jelly over one sheet of typing paper.
2. Light the candle and hold it below the coated side of the typing paper. **CAUTION:** *Be careful not to burn the paper or yourself. Keep hair and clothes away from open flame.*
3. Allow the carbon to coat the petroleum jelly on the paper. Extinguish the candle.
4. Place the fern frond on the carbon on the paper.
5. Cover the leaf with the paper towel and press gently.
6. Remove the towel and lift the leaf from the paper with the tweezers. Place the coated side of the leaf on the second sheet of paper. Press with the other paper towel.
7. Remove the towel and carefully remove the fern frond. Diagram your results under Data and Observations.

Data and Observations
Diagram fern frond here.

Questions and Conclusions

1. Is this a true carbon impression? _____ Explain. _____
   _____

2. Is there carbon in a frond before it becomes a fossil? _____ Explain. _____
   _____
   _____

3. Why is the carbon left in a true carbon impression? _____
   _____
   _____

4. In what type of climate would carbon impressions be more likely to form? _____
   Why? _____
   _____

Strategy Check

_____ Can you make a carbon impression of a fern frond?

NAME _____ DATE _____ CLASS _____

Chapter 13
LABORATORY MANUAL
● Geologic Time 36

Geologic time is divided into units, based on the presence or absence of certain forms of life. Before the record of past life began to appear in the rocks, many billions of years had passed. With the beginning of the Paleozoic Era, hard parts of animals began to be preserved in certain rocks. Some of our record is based on plants although they are not preserved as often as animal hard parts, such as shells, teeth, or even skeletons.

Strategy
You will construct a block diagram.
You will use the rock record to interpret the geologic map.
You will interpret the history and determine the ages of the rocks illustrated.

Materials
cardboard (thin)
glue or paste
geologic time scale, p. 358, *Glencoe Earth Science* © 1997
Figure 36-1
pencils (colored)
scissors
tape (clear)

Procedure
1. Glue the block diagram, Figure 36-1, to the cardboard.
2. Set up a legend and color code for the illustration. Record the legend in Table 36-1.
3. Cut out, fold, and tape the diagram to form a geologic map and four cross sections.

Data and Observations
Table 36-1
Legend for Rock Layers

Rock layers	Color
Layer A	
Layer B	
Layer C	
Layer D	

Copyright © Glencoe/McGraw-Hill, a division of The McGraw-Hill Companies, Inc.

Questions and Conclusions

1. During what period did the dike intrude into the rock sequence? _____

2. What is the probable age of the oldest layer shown? _____ Explain. _____
   _____
   _____

3. What is the probable age of the youngest layer shown? _____ Explain. _____
   _____
   _____

4. Is the dike older or younger than Layer E? _____ How can you tell? _____
   _____
   _____
   _____

5. Write a summary of the geologic history of this area. Try to name the periods of geologic time involved. _____
   _____
   _____
   _____
   _____

Strategy Check

_____ Can you construct a block diagram?

_____ Can you determine the age of an intrusion by its relative position?

_____ Can you write a geologic history of the area?

NAME	DATE	CLASS

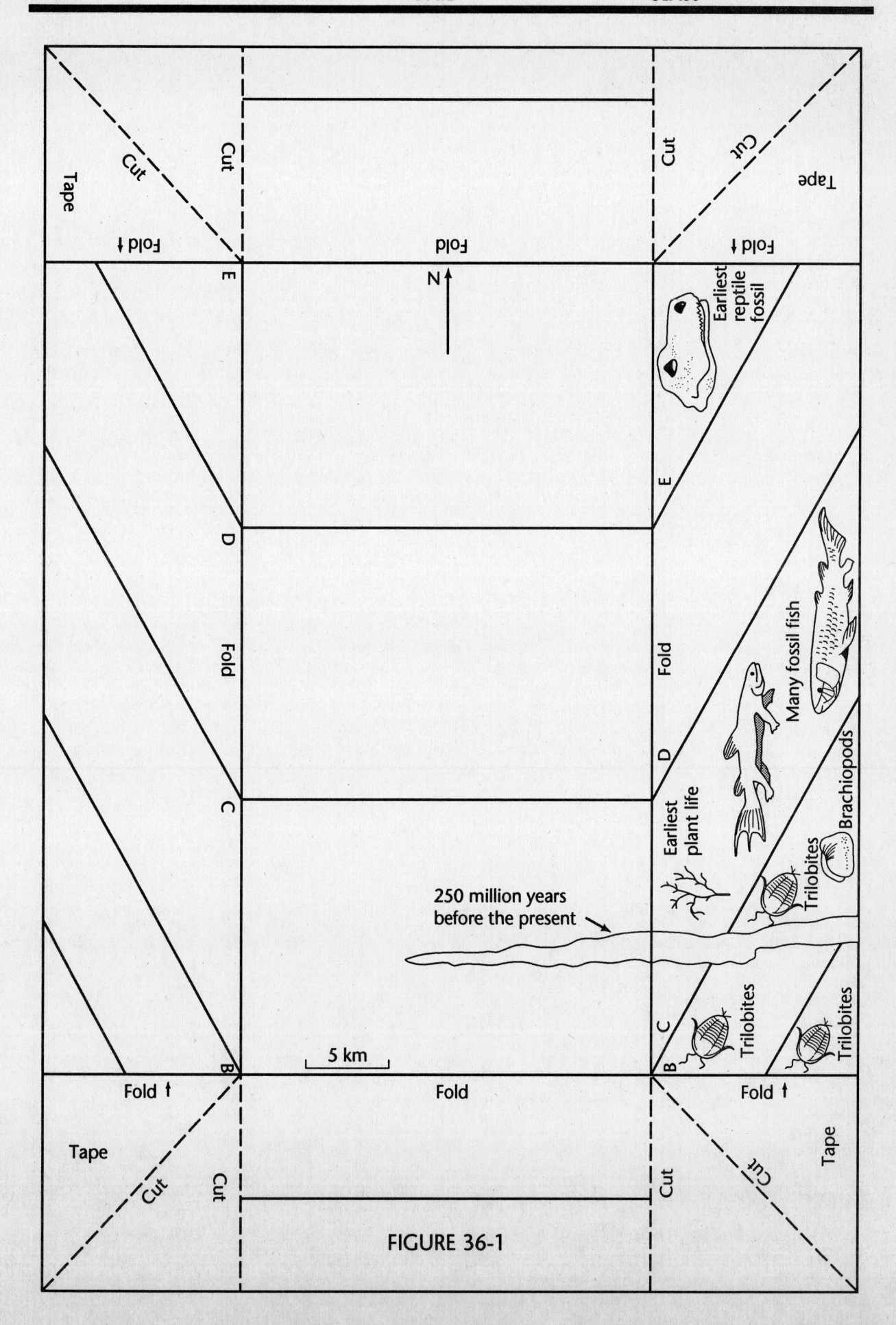

FIGURE 36-1

Labels visible on figure: Tape, Cut, Fold, N↑, E, D, C, B, Earliest reptile fossil, Many fossil fish, Earliest plant life, Brachiopods, Trilobites, 250 million years before the present, 5 km

Chapter 13
LABORATORY MANUAL
Differences in a Species 37

To use fossil dating efficiently, paleontologists first separate fossils into groups. The most useful group is called a species. A *species* is a population of individuals that have similar characteristics. Small differences in individuals may result in the development of a new species by a series of gradual changes. These changes can be traced from one geologic time division to another, if the fossil record is good.

Strategy
You will describe the variations present within a species.
You will describe a species in terms of one characteristic.

Materials
graph paper   meterstick   pencils (colored)

Procedure
1. The species you will study is *Homo sapiens,* or yourself. You and your classmates are all members of this species.
2. Record all characteristics of the species that you can. Record which of the characteristics you could measure and compare for all members of the species.
3. Measure and record in Table 37-1 the height of yourself and each of your classmates. Round off the height to the nearest decimeter (0.1 m).
4. Measure and record the heights of a class of younger students. Record in Table 37-2.

Data and Observations *(See page 96.)*

Questions and Conclusions
1. On what characteristics can you classify this group as a single species? _____

2. Where do most of the members of your class fall in regard to height? _____

3. Where do most of the members of the younger class fall in regard to height? _____

4. What change has taken place over time? _____

5. How is this activity like fossil dating? _____

   How is it different? (Hint: Think in terms of the time spans involved.) _____

Data and Observations

Characteristics: _____
_____
_____

Table 37-1

Person	Height (m)	Person	Height (m)

Table 37-2

Person	Height (m)	Person	Height (m)

Graph the Frequency (number of persons having the same height) on the vertical axis against the Height (m) on the horizontal axis. Use one color for your own class and a second color for the younger class.

Strategy Check

_____ Can you describe the variations present within a species?

_____ Can you describe a species in terms of a range of a characteristic?

NAME _____ DATE _____ CLASS _____

Chapter 14
LABORATORY MANUAL
Air 38

Earth's atmosphere is made up primarily of air. You can't always see it, but air is real! Like any other form of matter, air has definite physical properties. As you work through this activity, you will observe two of the properties of air—volume and pressure.

Strategy
You will demonstrate that air has volume (occupies space).
You will demonstrate that air exerts pressure.

Materials
air mattress   bicycle pump   water
beaker (500 mL)   meterstick

Procedure
1. Put 250 mL of water in the beaker.

2. Insert the hose of the bicycle pump so it is below the surface of the water.

3. To demonstrate that air occupies space, pump air into the water. Record your observations. Remove the pump hose.

4. To demonstrate that air exerts pressure, place the air mattress on the floor. Press the mattress flat to be sure it contains very little air. Feel the floor through the mattress.

5. Measure in centimeters the length, width, and thickness of the air mattress. Record your measurements in Table 38-1 on page 98.

6. Inflate the mattress using the bicycle pump. Remeasure and record the dimensions.

7. Push down with your hand on one area of the inflated air mattress. Note how the dimensions of the area that you are pushing on change. How does the part of the mattress surrounding your hands change?

Data and Observations

Observations:
Air pumped into beaker _____
_____

Pushing down on mattress _____
_____

Table 38-1

Air Mattress	Before pumping	After pumping
Length (cm)		
Width (cm)		
Thickness (cm)		

Questions and Conclusions

1. What happened in the beaker of water when you pumped air into it? _____
_____

2. What property of air does this demonstrate? _____
_____

3. Calculate the volume of air in the air mattress. Show your work in the box below. If you need more room, use the back of this page.

4. What happened to the thickness of the air mattress in the area where you pushed on it?
_____

5. What happened to the area of the air mattress surrounding the area you pushed? What property of air does this show? _____
_____

6. Does air exert pressure? _____ Defend your answer. _____
_____
_____

Strategy Check

____ Can you demonstrate that air has volume?

____ Can you demonstrate that air exerts pressure?

Chapter 14
LABORATORY MANUAL
Air Pressure 39

Air pressure results from the impact of air particles on an area. At sea level, the amount of air pressure pressing down against the ground is about 14.7 pounds per square inch. Air pressure is affected by temperature. The warmer the air, the more its particles move. The air becomes less dense and takes up more space. When air is less dense, it exerts a lower air pressure. As heat is removed from air particles, its particles move less and take up less space. Air pressure increases. Cooler air in the atmosphere exerts a higher air pressure. Changes in air pressure often affect the weather.

Meteorologists and other weather watchers use a *barometer* to measure air pressure. Mercury (Hg) barometers measure the air pressure in inches of mercury. Using this kind of barometer, the air pressure at sea level measures about 29.92 inches (760 mm) of mercury. By observing a barometer, a person can predict how the weather may or may not change.

Strategy
You will demonstrate how the temperature of air affects air pressure.
You will measure air pressure over a period of time.
You will graph your data and compare your graph with those of your classmates.

Materials
2 balloons
barometer (aneroid or mercury)
2 empty beverage or condiment bottles
graph paper

ice
2 pans or large bowls
water (hot and cold)

Procedure
1. Attach a balloon over the top of each empty bottle. Place one bottle in a bowl or pan containing hot water. Place the other bottle in a bowl or pan containing cold water and ice. Record your observations under Data and Observations on page 100.

2. Record the air pressure three times each day for a week. Be sure to read the barometer at the same times each day. Record your data in Table 39-1.

3. Record any other observations of the weather also. Record all data in Table 39-1.

FIGURE 39-1

Data and Observations *(See page 100.)*

Questions and Conclusions

1. Explain the changes in both balloons in terms of air temperature and air pressure. _____
   _____
   _____
   _____

2. Do you see any patterns in your barometric pressure data? _____
   Explain. _____
   _____

3. Do these patterns agree with patterns observed by your classmates? _____
   Explain. _____

Data and Observations

Balloon observations _____
_____
_____

Table 39-1

Date	Time	Barometric pressure	Other	Date	Time	Barometric pressure	Other
	1. 2. 3.				1. 2. 3.		
	1. 2. 3.				1. 2. 3.		
	1. 2. 3.						

Graph your barometric pressure data, Pressure vs. Time. Graph Pressure on the vertical axis and Time on the horizontal axis.

Strategy Check

_____ Can you demonstrate how the temperature of air affects air pressure?

_____ Can you measure air pressure?

_____ Can you graph your data?

Chapter 14
LABORATORY MANUAL
Temperature of the Air 40

Air temperature is a fundamental variable important to the scientific study of weather. Air temperature affects air pressure, and thus the type of weather that may occur. Differences in air temperature also cause the winds. By studying the air temperature and weather at different times during the day, you may be able to predict how the air temperature will affect the local weather.

Strategy
You will measure the air temperature at different times during the day.
You will measure the air temperature at the same location each time.
You will graph your results and compare your graph with those of your classmates.

Materials
Celsius thermometer (metal backed)
graph paper

Procedure
1. Select an outdoor site for taking air temperature readings. Make sure the site is an open shaded area.
2. Record the air temperature at this site three times each day for a week. Be careful to read the thermometer at the same times each day. Record data in Table 40-1.
3. Record additional weather factors, such as cloud cover, precipitation, and winds.

Data and Observations
Table 40-1

Date	Time	Temp (°C)	Other	Date	Time	Temp (°C)	Other
	1. 2. 3.				1. 2. 3.		
	1. 2. 3.				1. 2. 3.		
	1. 2. 3.						

Graph your data showing Temperature against Time. Graph the Temperature on the vertical axis and the Time on the horizontal axis.

Questions and Conclusions

1. Why did you take your air temperature readings in the shade instead of in the sun? _____
   _____
   _____

2. Do you see any patterns in your air temperature graph? _____ What patterns?
   _____

3. Do these patterns agree with patterns observed by your classmates? _____
   Explain. _____

4. How can you explain the patterns in terms of solar energy absorbed by the land? _____
   _____
   _____
   _____
   _____

Strategy Check

_____ Can you measure air temperature?

_____ Can you collect data for a week?

_____ Can you graph your data?

NAME _____ DATE _____ CLASS _____

Chapter 14
LABORATORY MANUAL

Air in Motion 41

Winds are horizontal air movements caused by temperature differences among masses of air. To identify winds, people label them according to the direction from which they blow. Winds are not only responsible for the movement of weather around the world, they also affect local weather. You can use a wind vane to see how local wind direction changes are related to local weather changes.

Strategy

You will build a simple wind vane.
You will observe and record wind directions.

Materials

compass (Figure 41-2)
hammer
plastic (thin and stiff—15 cm x 15 cm)
scissors
straight pin
straw (plastic)
tape (clear)
washer
wood block, 5 cm x 5 cm x 45 cm

Procedure

1. Make a small slit in each end of the drinking straw by cutting the straw with a scissors. The slit at the arrow end of the straw should be about 3 cm. The slit at the tail end of the straw should be about 5 cm. NOTE: Make sure the slits align with each other.

2. Cut a small arrow and large tail for the wind vane. Make sure the arrow is long and narrow. Follow the example in Figure 41-1. Insert the arrow and tail into the slits in the straw. Secure the arrow and tail with a small amount of tape.

3. Using your finger, find the point on the straw where the two halves balance. NOTE: This will *not* be in the center of the straw. When you find this point, poke the straight pin through the straw, as shown in Figure 41-1. Enlarge the hole slightly so that the straw can turn freely.

4. Cut out Figure 41-2 and tape to the wood block. Using the hammer, gently drive the pin through the washer and into the center of the compass.

5. Place the vane in the wind in a large, open area.

7. Hold the wind vane so that the *N* on the block points north. Note the position of the pointer on your wind vane. Use the compass to determine the direction of wind movement.

8. Record the wind direction three times a day, each day for a week. Record the wind direction at the same time each day. Record your data in Table 41-1.

9. Record any other weather observations in Table 41-1.

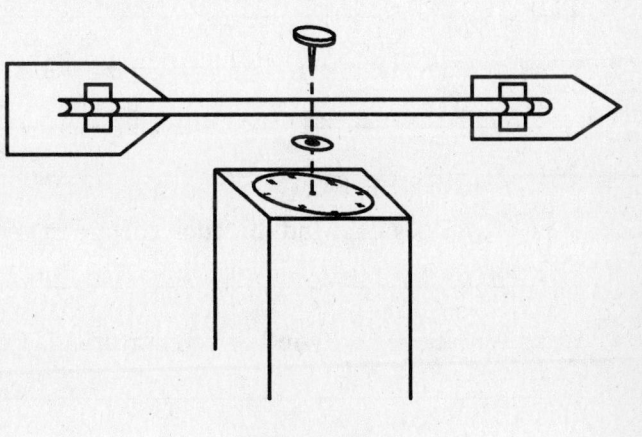

FIGURE 41-1

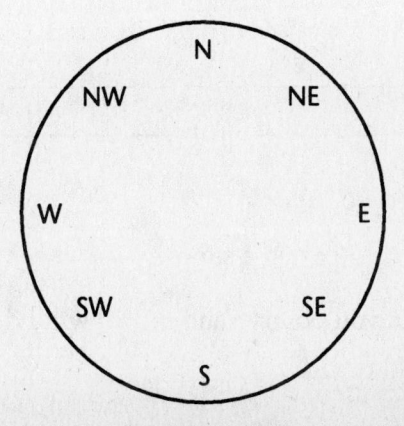

FIGURE 41-2

Data and Observations

Table 41-1

Date	Time	Wind direction	Other	Date	Time	Wind direction	Other
	1. 2. 3.				1. 2. 3.		
	1. 2. 3.				1. 2. 3.		
	1. 2. 3.						

Questions and Conclusions

1. Why does the arrow of a wind vane point into the wind? _____

2. Why is the arrow long and narrow on the wind vane? _____

3. How often does the wind direction change in your area? _____

4. Weather stations take wind direction readings from the tops of tall buildings or high poles. Why? _____

5. Do you see any relationship between the wind direction and weather?
   What is that relationship? _____

Strategy Check

____ Can you build a simple wind vane?

____ Can you observe and record wind directions?

NAME _____ DATE _____ CLASS _____

Chapter 15
LABORATORY MANUAL
• Wind Power 42

Wind is an important renewable energy source. Some of the solar radiation that strikes Earth's atmosphere is changed to heat energy. The alternate heating and cooling of the atmosphere as Earth rotates causes air pressure differences. Wind energy can be used to drive generators to produce electricity. Any wind that blows at a constant speed of over 12.8 kilometers per hour can be used to generate electricity. However, the efficiency of the wind as an energy source depends also on the generating system.

Strategy
You will construct a simple device to measure wind speed.
You will measure the wind speed at different times during the day for a week.
You will evaluate wind as a source of energy.

Materials
cardboard (stiff)
colored marker
glue or paste
graph paper
needle long enough to go through ball
nylon line, 30 cm
Ping-Pong ball
scissors

Procedure
1. Cut out the protractor in Figure 42-2 and glue it to the cardboard.
2. Thread the nylon line through the needle and push the needle through the center of the Ping-Pong ball.
3. Tie a knot in the end of the nylon line and glue it to the ball. Glue the free end of the nylon line to the spot marked Center on the protractor.
4. Color the nylon line with the colored marker.
5. Test the device by setting it on the edge of the desk. If it is level, the line should cover the 0° mark.
6. Select the windiest area of the school grounds. Block the wind and level the device. See Figure 42-1. Hold the device level and face the wind. Allow the wind to move the Ping-Pong ball. The angle made by the nylon line will be the wind speed in degrees. Measure the angle and record it in Table 42-1.
7. Measure and record the wind speed in degrees three times a day for a week. Use the same site each time. Record your measurements in Table 42-1.

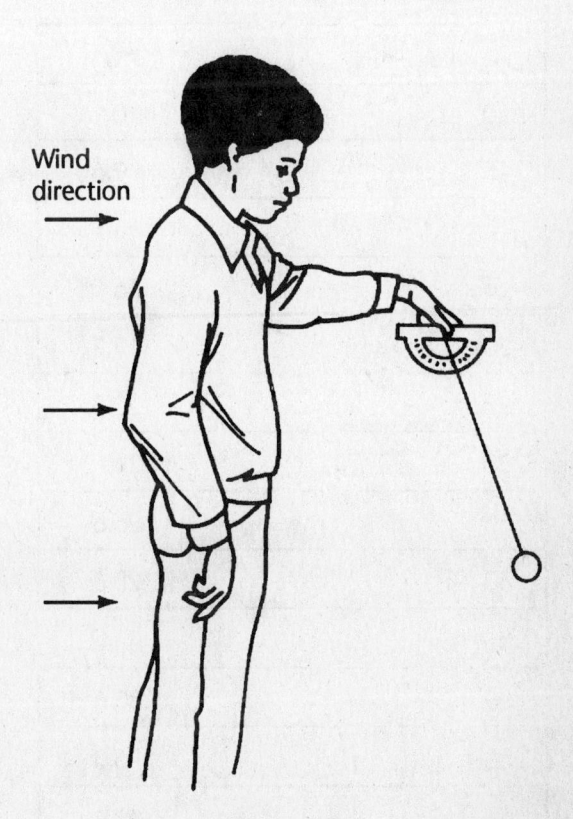

FIGURE 42-1

Copyright © Glencoe/McGraw-Hill, a division of The McGraw-Hill Companies, Inc.

105

Data and Observations

Table 42-1

Date/Time	Wind speed (°)	Wind speed in km/h	Date/Time	Wind speed (°)	Wind speed in km/h

Use Table 42-2 and convert your Wind speed in degrees to Wind speed in kilometers per hour. Fill in the column in Table 42-1.

Graph the Wind speed in kilometers per hour on the vertical axis of the graph paper and graph Date/Time on the horizontal axis.

Table 42-2

Angle	km/h
0	0
5	9.6
10	13
15	16
20	19.2
25	20.8
30	24
35	25.6
40	28.8
45	32
50	33.6
55	36.8
60	41.6
65	46.4
70	52.8

NAME _____ DATE _____ CLASS _____

Questions and Conclusions

1. Is the wind constant in your area? _____ What effect does this have on electric generation? _____
_____

2. Estimate how many hours a day you could generate electricity at your site. _____
_____

3. What are some advantages to the use of wind power to generate electricity? _____
_____
_____

4. What are some drawbacks to using wind power? _____
_____
_____

Strategy Check

_____ Can you construct a device to measure wind speed?

_____ Can you measure wind speed?

_____ Can you evaluate wind as a source of energy?

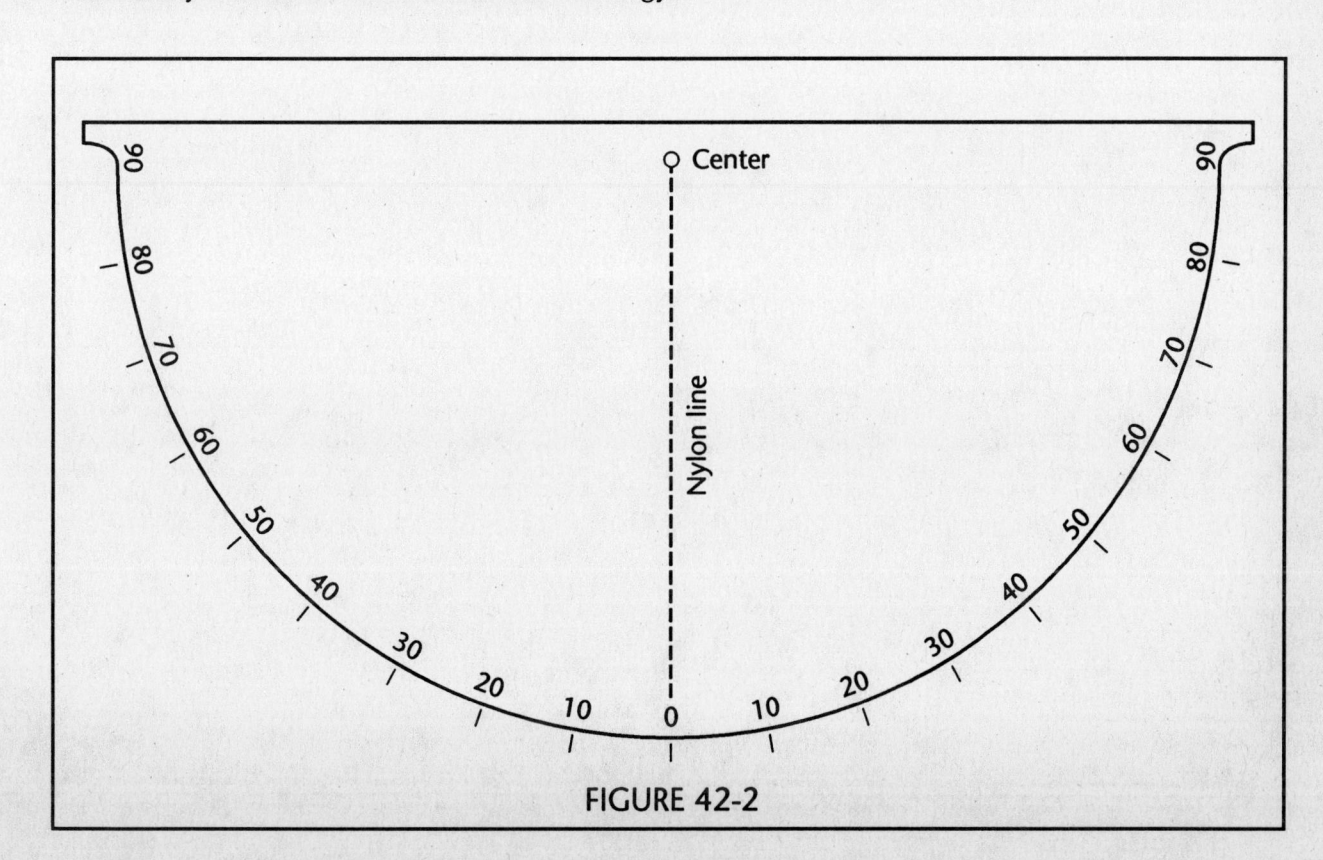

FIGURE 42-2

NAME _____ DATE _____ CLASS _____

Chapter 15
LABORATORY MANUAL • Clouds 43

Clouds are tiny droplets of water or crystals of ice suspended in the air. There are three basic cloud forms: cirrus, stratus, and cumulus. Clouds are also classified by their height above ground level. High clouds are designated by the prefix *cirro*, and middle clouds by the prefix *alto*. Low clouds have no prefix. Clouds that produce precipitation have the prefix *nimbo* or the suffix *nimbus* added. A cirrostratus cloud is a high, layered cloud. A nimbostratus cloud is a low, layered, precipitation-producing cloud.

Clouds often indicate weather changes. By learning to recognize the different kinds of clouds and their relative positions in the sky, you sometimes can predict the coming weather.

Strategy
You will observe and identify clouds.
You will observe and record the weather associated with the clouds.

Materials
"Cloud Code Chart" (pictures and/or descriptions of clouds)

Procedure
1. Observe and record the cloud cover and cloud type once a day for a week. Try to make your observations at the same time each day. Observe and record the general weather also. Record all data in Table 43-1.

2. Estimate cloud cover. Record the cloud cover using the following symbols and abbreviations:
   - CLF = Free of clouds
   - SCT = Scattered clouds (half or less of sky covered)
   - BKN = Broken clouds (more than half of sky covered, but blue still showing through)
   - OVC = Overcast (no blue visible)
   - X = Obscured (fog, smoke, or haze completely covers the sky)

3. Use the following symbols to record the type(s) of clouds you observe:
   - Ci—Cirrus
   - Cu—Cumulus
   - St—Stratus
   - Cb—Cumulonimbus
   - Ns—Nimbostratus
   - Ac—Altocumulus
   - As—Altostratus

Data and Observations

Table 43-1

Date	Time	Cloud cover	Cloud type	Weather

Questions and Conclusions

1. Based on your observations, write a description of each of the three basic cloud forms.

   _____

   _____

   _____

   _____

   _____

2. What type of weather is associated with cirrus clouds? _____

3. What type of weather is associated with cumulonimbus clouds? _____

4. What type of weather is associated with cumulus clouds? _____

5. What type of weather is associated with nimbostratus clouds? _____

Strategy Check

_____ Can you observe and identify clouds?

_____ Can you observe and record weather?

NAME _____ DATE _____ CLASS _____

Chapter 15

LABORATORY MANUAL • **Hurricanes 44**

Hurricanes are violent storms that form over water in the zone of the Trade Winds. They produce strong winds, high seas, and heavy rain and if they reach land do great damage. When winds reach an intensity of 63 to 117 kilometers per hour, the disturbance is called a tropical storm. But when winds exceed 117 kilometers per hour, the disturbance is called a hurricane if it is in the Atlantic Ocean, Caribbean Sea, or Gulf of Mexico. The term *hurricane* comes from an American Indian word that means "big wind." If this type of storm forms in the North Pacific, it is called a typhoon.

The U.S. Weather Bureau begins reporting a *hurricane watch* when a hurricane reaches a position where it appears likely to endanger land areas. The watch begins a few days before the hurricane is expected to reach land. This gives people an opportunity to take the necessary steps to protect their lives and property. *Hurricane warning* means that all precautions should be taken immediately because your area is expected to be in the path of the hurricane. Hurricanes sometimes take unexpected course changes, which makes them especially dangerous.

Strategy
You will plot the paths of two hurricanes.
You will compare the paths of the two hurricanes.

Materials
pencils (colored—red, blue)

Procedure
1. On the hurricane tracking chart on page 113, plot the path of Hurricane Doria for each day. Plot the path with the red pencil. Use the data in Table 44-1.
2. On the same hurricane tracking chart, plot the path of Hurricane Betsy for each day. Plot the path with the blue pencil. Use the data in Table 44-2.
3. Compare the paths of the two hurricanes.

Data and Observations *(See page 113.)*

Questions and Conclusions
1. Where did Betsy hit land? _____
2. Where did Doria hit land? _____
3. In which general direction, north or south, do hurricanes move? _____
4. Why do you think hurricanes form over water? _____
5. Which areas of the United States are in the most danger from hurricanes? _____
6. What type of damage is caused by a hurricane? _____

Table 44-1. Hurricane Doria

Date (September 1967)	Position (at 7 A.M.) Latitude	Position (at 7 A.M.) Longitude
9	27.5°N	79°W
10	30.5°N	77.5°W
11	36°N	71°W
12	36°N	66°W
13	36.5°N	64.5°W
14	37.5°N	65.5°W
15	38.5°N	68°W
16	38°N	74.5°W
17	36°N	76°W

Table 44-2. Hurricane Betsy

Date (August–September 1965)	Position (at 7 A.M.) Latitude	Position (at 7 A.M.) Longitude
29	19.5°N	63.5°W
30	22.5°N	65.5°W
31	23°N	66.5°W
1	21°N	67°W
2	23.5°N	70°W
3	26°N	73°W
4	28°N	75°W
5	28.5°N	76°W
6	29.5°N	76°W
7	25.5°N	78°W
8	25.5°N	81°W
9	26.5°N	87°W
10	29.5°N	90.5°W
11	33°N	92°W

Strategy Check

_____ Can you plot the path of a hurricane?

_____ Can you compare the paths of two hurricanes?

NAME _____ DATE _____ CLASS _____

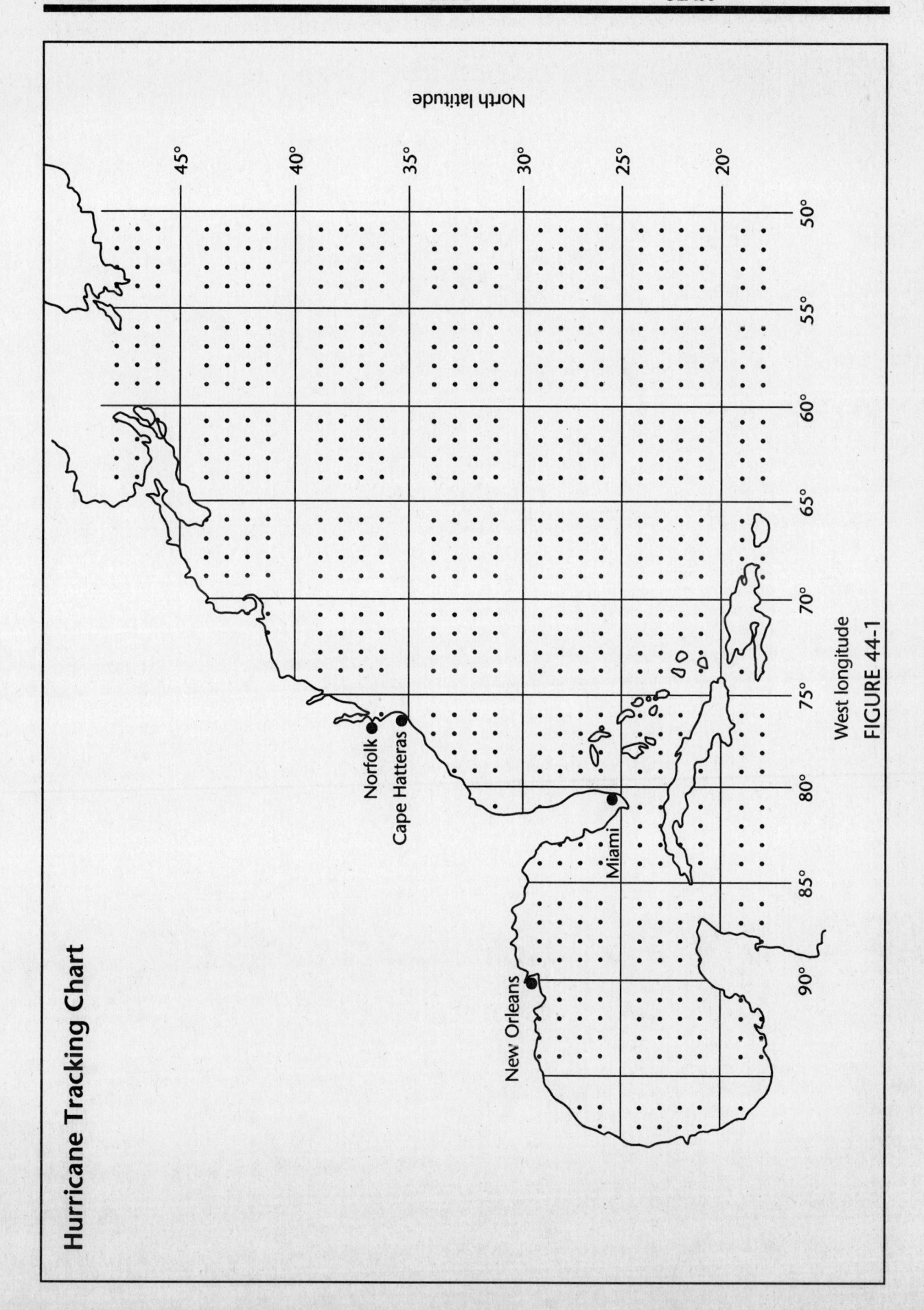

Hurricane Tracking Chart

FIGURE 44-1

Chapter 15
LABORATORY MANUAL
Weather Forecasting 45

Weather includes a variety of short term changes in pressure, temperature, wind direction, cloud formation, and amounts of water vapor in the air. Forecasting is a very complex and challenging occupation. Forecasting involves observing, analyzing, and predicting the interrelationships among the sun's energy, the physical features of Earth, and the properties of the atmosphere.

Strategy
You will compile weather data collected over a period of time.
You will analyze the data for patterns.
You will predict the coming weather based on your analysis of the data.

Materials
charts from Activity 39, Activity 40, Activity 41, Activity 43
graph paper
pencils (colored)

Procedure
1. Complete Table 45-1 using the data from the charts in Activity 39, Activity 40, Activity 41, Activity 43, and Appendix J, page 719.
2. Graph Air Temperature vs. Time on a piece of graph paper. Using the same graph, plot Air Pressure vs. Time.
3. Reread all of the notes you made in Activity 39, Activity 40, Activity 41, and Activity 43. Think about how the things you observed can help you predict the weather.

Data and Observations (See page 116.)

Questions and Conclusions
1. Why was it important for you to collect all of your data within a particular time span? _____
_____
_____

2. What relationship did you find between rapid changes in air temperatures and the weather?
_____
_____
_____

3. What is the relationship between air pressure and weather? _____
_____
_____

4. Forecast the weather for your area for the next two days. _____
_____
_____

Data and Observations

Table 45-1

Date/Time	Weather (fog, rain, snow)	Air pressure	Air temperature	Wind direction	Clouds/ Cloud cover

Strategy Check

____ Can you compile data?

____ Can you analyze data?

____ Can you predict the weather?

NAME _____ DATE _____ CLASS _____

Chapter 16
LABORATORY MANUAL
Radiant Energy and Climate 46

The amount of radiant energy received from the sun depends on the angle at which the energy strikes Earth. The energy strikes the equator at about 90° relative to the horizon. At the poles, the energy strikes Earth at a very low angle. Climates can be classified according to the amount of radiant energy received by Earth in a given area.

Strategy
You will demonstrate that the angle at which radiant energy strikes Earth controls the amount of radiation received.
You will deduce the relationship between the amount of radiant energy an area receives and its climate.

Materials
flashlight   pencils (red, blue, black, pink, light blue, gray)
graph paper   protractor

Procedure
1. Place the graph paper flat on the desk.
2. Position the flashlight 20 cm directly above the paper so it shines at 90° to the paper.
3. Outline the area of intense light using the red pencil. Outline the area of less intense light using the pink pencil.
4. Hold the flashlight at 45° to the paper and 20 cm above it. Be sure the light shines on a clean area of the graph paper. Outline the area of intense light in dark blue, and the area of less intense light in light blue.
5. Hold the flashlight at 3° to the paper and 20 cm above it. Outline the area of intense light in black, and the area of less intense light in gray.

Questions and Conclusions
1. List the areas of most intense energy in order of size from largest to smallest. _____
_____
_____

2. List the areas of less intense energy in order of size from largest to smallest. _____
_____
_____

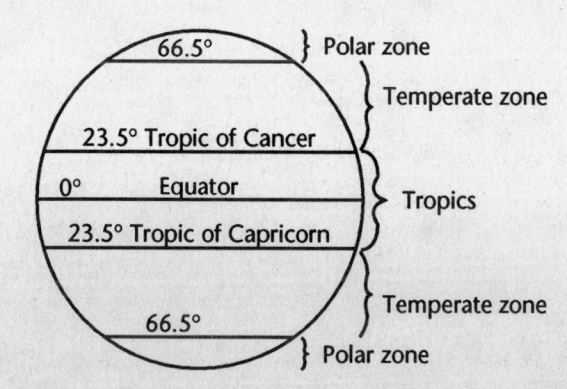

FIGURE 46-1

Copyright © Glencoe/McGraw-Hill, a division of The McGraw-Hill Companies, Inc.

3. What climate zone does each radiant energy zone represent? _____
_____
_____

4. Based on this activity, which climate zone would you expect to have the warmest temperatures? Explain. _____
_____
_____
_____
_____

5. Describe the type of climate of each of the three zones. _____
_____
_____
_____

Strategy Check

____ Can you demonstrate that the angle at which radiant energy strikes Earth controls the amount of radiation received?

____ Can you deduce the relationship between climate and the amount of radiant energy an area receives?

Chapter 16
LABORATORY MANUAL
Solar Energy Storage 47

Solar energy is not always available when we need it, such as on cloudy days and at night. Storing the solar energy is one of the problems that must be solved before solar energy can be used on a large scale. One method of storage involves solids such as rocks. Another method involves the use of water or air.

Strategy
You will construct storage tanks for heat energy.
You will compare the ability of air and rocks to absorb and release heat energy.
You will explain how these storage methods can be used to heat a home.

Materials
beaker tongs or pliers
2 small coffee cans with lids
graph paper
gravel
hot plate
pencils (colored)
2 thermometers
watch with second hand
water

Procedure
1. Fill one coffee can half full of water and set it on the hot plate. Measure the water's temperature near the bottom of the can and near the top. Record the temperatures in Table 47-1.

2. Turn the hot plate to high and allow it to heat for two minutes. Measure the temperature of the water near the bottom of the can and close to the top every minute for fifteen minutes. Record the temperatures in Table 47-1. **CAUTION:** *Do not leave thermometer in can during heating.*

3. Remove the can with water. **CAUTION:** *Hot water can cause serious burns. Allow the hot plate to cool.*

4. Fill the second coffee can half full of gravel and place it on the hot plate. Measure the temperature near the bottom and top of the can. Record the temperatures in Table 47-1.

5. Repeat Step 2. Allow the can with the gravel to remain on the hot plate until it is completely cool.

Data and Observations (See page 120.)

Questions and Conclusions
1. Which material heated more rapidly? _____ How do you know? _____

2. Which material cooled more rapidly? _____ How do you know? _____

3. Which material would you choose to store heat energy from a solar collector? _____
   Explain. _____

4. If you use a solar collector that circulates water, you need a large tank of water to store the heat, generally 2.7 liters per square meter. How much water would you need to store to heat a house with an area of 1380 square meters? _____

5. How would you store the rocks necessary for a solid solar storage system? _____
_____

6. How can you change the storage system to make it more efficient than it is in this activity?
_____
_____

Data and Observations

Table 47-1

Time (min)	Temperature (°C)				
	Water		Gravel	
	Top	Bottom	Top	Bottom

Graph the Temperature vs. Time for each material. Use a different colored pencil for each graph.

Strategy Check

____ Can you construct tanks for heat energy?

____ Can you compare the capability of gravel and water to absorb and release heat energy?

____ Can you see how these storage methods can be used to heat a home?

Chapter 16
LABORATORY MANUAL
Solar Energy Application 48

Many homes in this country now use solar energy to heat all or part of their water. A solar water heater consists of a solar collector, a storage tank, and regular plumbing. An efficient solar water heater can provide 4.1 liters of hot water per 0.1 square meters of collector surface on a sunny day.

Strategy
You will construct a small solar water heater.
You will design a solar water heating system for your home.

Materials
beaker (50 mL)
cardboard box, shallow
clamp (to hold condensation column)
condensation column
funnel
glass plate large enough to cover box
glycerol
paint (flat black spray)

pinch clamp
ring stand
stopper (1-hole to fit condensation column)
thermometer
tubing (black rubber, 600 cm)
watch with second hand
water

Procedure
1. Paint the inside of the box black.
2. Set up the equipment as shown in Figure 48-1. **CAUTION:** *Be sure to moisten the funnel stem with glycerol before inserting it into the stopper.*

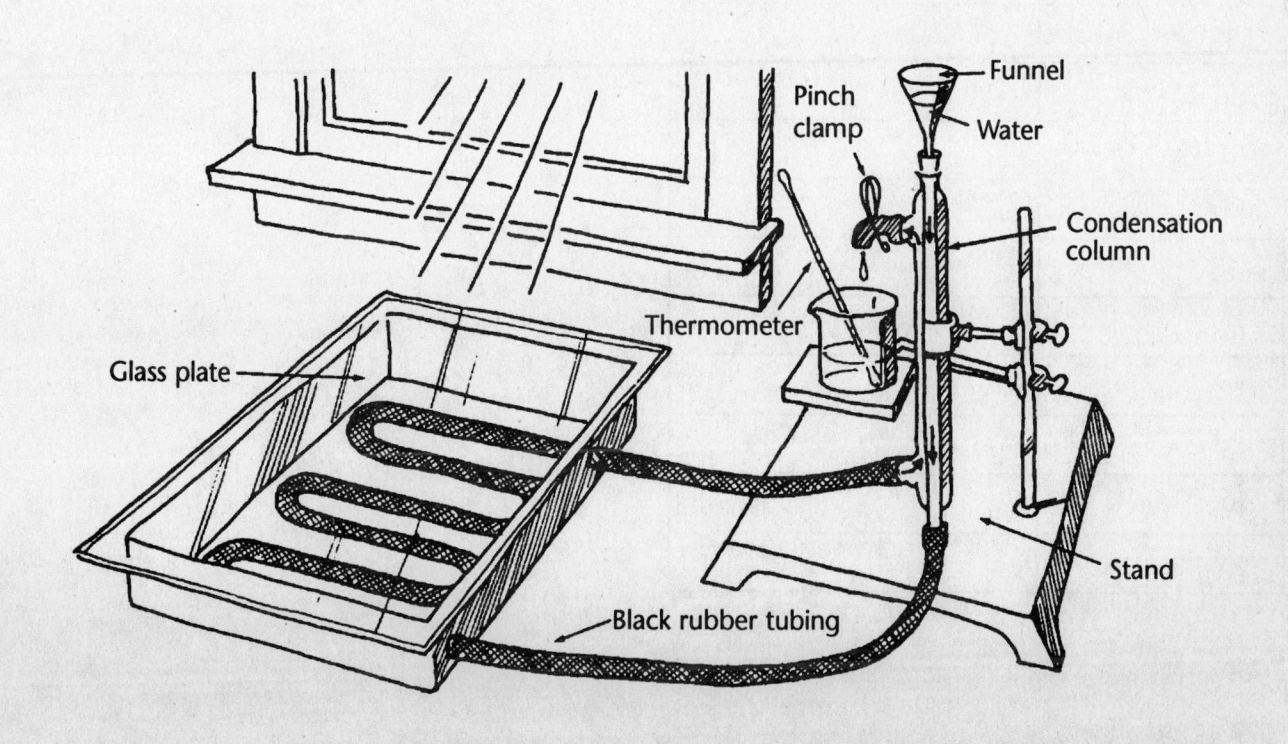

3. Fill the unit with water. Be sure the tubing and the condensation column are completely filled.
4. Run 50 mL of water into the beaker and measure the temperature. Record. Pour the water back into the funnel. **CAUTION:** *Be careful handling hot water.*
5. Place the unit in the sun and measure the water temperature each minute for 20 minutes. Record the temperatures in Table 48-1. NOTE: Be sure to pour the water sample back into the system each time.

Data and Observations

Table 48-1

Time (min)	Temperature (°C)
0	
1	
2	
3	
4	
5	
6	
7	
8	
9	
10	
11	
12	
13	
14	
15	
16	
17	
18	
19	
20	

Questions and Conclusions

1. How hot does the water become? _____ How long did it take to reach this temperature? _____

2. Why did the temperature level off? _____

3. Where does the energy to heat the water come from? _____

4. Why did you use a black tube? _____

5. Would the water heat up if the tubing were not in a solar collector? _____ Explain. _____

6. Where would the collector box be placed in a home solar water heating system? _____

7. Which part of this equipment corresponds to the water heater tank in your home? _____ Which part is like the cold water pipe? _____

8. How could you modify the equipment used here to produce a higher temperature in a shorter time? _____

9. Why did you paint the inside of the box black? _____

10. Predict the results of the activity if you had painted the inside of the box blue. Explain your predictions. _____

11. Draw a sketch of your home and surroundings in the space below. On the drawing, indicate the position of trees and any other sunscreens. Show where you would place a solar collector for your home. Write a paragraph defending your choice of location. Also, describe any problems that you can see with the chosen site.

_____
_____
_____
_____
_____

Strategy Check

____ Can you build a solar water heater?

____ Can you design a solar water heating system for your home?

Chapter 17
LABORATORY MANUAL

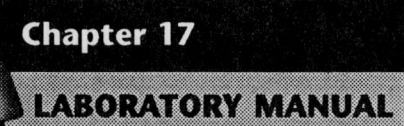

Salt Concentration in Ocean Water 49

Water in the oceans contains about 3.5 percent salts by weight. Ocean water is salty because water on land dissolves elements such as calcium, magnesium, and sodium on its journey to the oceans. Elements such as sulfur and chlorine are brought to the oceans as a result of erupting volcanoes. Sodium and chlorine, nearly 90 percent of the substances dissolved in ocean water, are what make up table salt. The oceans constantly receive salts and minerals. However, because these substances are used by life forms in the oceans, and they precipitate out, the oceans have not gotten saltier over millions of years.

Strategy
You will consider the effects of a large concentration of salt in soil.
You will make a model showing how salt concentration in a portion of ocean water could increase.

Materials
beaker (100-mL)
flask (heat proof)
heat lamp
hot plate
plastic storage box (clear)
salt
sand (coarse)
towel
water
obtain from teacher a stopper with glass or plastic tubing inserted

Procedure
Part A
1. Mix 100 mL of salt with 100 mL of sand. Pour the mixture into the bottom of the storage box. Add enough water to dissolve the salt. Cover this mixture with a layer of sand five centimeters thick.

2. Set the box under the heat lamp or in a sunny location. Allow the box to remain undisturbed overnight.

3. Record your observations, including a sketch, in Table 49-1.

Part B
1. Dissolve 10 mL of salt in 50 mL of water and pour it into the flask. Record the volume of "ocean water" in Table 49-2.

2. Set up the distillation apparatus as shown in Figure 49-1.

3. Place the flask on the hot plate. Slowly boil the water until all the water has evaporated.

4. Record the volume of water recovered in the beaker in Table 49-2.

5. Record the appearance of the bottom of the flask under "Observations" in Table 49-2.

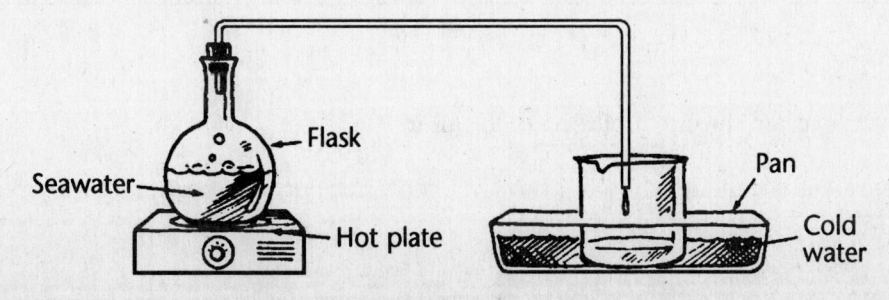

FIGURE 49-1

Data and Observations

Table 49-1

Observations: _____	
_____	
_____	
_____	

Table 49-2

Volume of salt water: _____ mL	Observations: _____
	_____
Volume of water recovered: _____ mL	_____

Questions and Conclusions

1. If a stream flowed through the sand and salt mixture, what would happen to the salt? _____
_____

2. In areas that use river water for irrigation, how could salt become a problem? _____
_____

3. Explain how the salt content of the ocean could start to increase over time. _____
_____
_____

4. Why is the distillation of ocean water on a large scale not profitable? _____
_____

5. On a windy and rainy day the air tastes salty. What does this tell you about salt in the water cycle near oceans? _____
_____

Strategy Check

_____ Can you explain the effect of too much salt in soil?

_____ Can you make a model showing how salt concentration in a portion of the ocean could increase?

Chapter 17
LABORATORY MANUAL
Fresh Water from Ocean Water 50

Many natural processes add to the mineral content of ocean water and density currents. One natural process helps to concentrate minerals in the lower levels of the water. This process is freezing. As ocean water freezes, the upper levels of ice are mostly pure water.

Strategy
You will demonstrate that freezing purifies ocean water.
You will consider the implication of this process for commercial use.

Materials
balance
freezer
4 freezer boxes
marking pencil
ocean water (salt water—make solution with salt and water)
4 paper cups
4 watch glasses

Procedure
1. Pour 250 mL of ocean water into a freezer container. Set in the freezer.
2. Place a small sample of ocean water in a paper cup. Label the cup 1.
3. When one-half of the water in the container is frozen, remove the container from the freezer.
4. Rinse the ice in water and place the ice in a second freezer container. Allow the ice to melt.
5. Place a sample of this water into a paper cup and label the cup 2.
6. Put the container into the freezer. When one-half of the water is ice, remove the container.
7. Repeat Steps 4, 5, and 6 twice. Be sure to label the cups in the correct order.
8. Label the watch glasses 1, 2, 3, and 4. Determine the mass of each watch glass and record in Table 50-1.
9. Place a sample of water from cup 1 on watch glass 1 and so on for all the samples. Use samples of equal size.
10. Allow the watch glasses to stand undisturbed until all the water has evaporated, leaving residue at the bottom of each glass.
11. Find the mass of each watch glass with the residue. Record the masses in Table 50-1.
12. Subtract the mass of each empty watch glass from the mass of the same watch glass with residue. Your result in each case will be the mass of the residue. Record the masses in Table 50-1.

Data and Observations

Table 50-1

	Mass of empty watch glass (g)	Mass of watch glass with residue (g)	Mass of residue (g)
1			
2			
3			
4			
5			

Questions and Conclusions

1. What happened to the salt during successive freezings? _____
_____
_____

2. How much salt would you expect to find in glaciers at Earth's poles? _____
_____

3. Discuss the pros and cons of freezing seawater to obtain fresh water. _____
_____
_____
_____

Strategy Check

_____ Can you demonstrate that freezing purifies ocean water?

_____ Can you see advantages and disadvantages of freezing ocean water on a commercial scale?

NAME _____ DATE _____ CLASS _____

Chapter 17
LABORATORY MANUAL

Density Currents 51

Some ocean currents are set in motion by differences in the density of the water from place to place. These density differences are caused by differences in the water temperature and/or the amount of dissolved salts in the water.

Strategy
You will determine the effect of temperature on the density of water.
You will determine the effects of the amount of dissolved salt on the density of water.
You will set a density current in motion.
You will explain how density currents form in the ocean.

Materials
2 baby food jars   dishpan   stirring rod
beaker (1000 mL)   food coloring   water (hot and cold)
cardboard (stiff)   salt

Procedure
1. Fill one baby food jar with hot water. Add a few drops of food coloring. Set the jar in the dishpan.
2. Fill the second jar with cold water. Place the cardboard firmly over the top of the jar.
3. Hold the cardboard in place and carefully turn the jar of cold water upside down over the jar of hot water. NOTE: Be sure the openings of the two jars match exactly.
4. Carefully remove the cardboard. Record your observations in Table 51-1.
5. Repeat Steps 1 and 2. This time put the cardboard over the jar of hot water.
6. Carefully invert the jar of hot water over the jar of cold water.
7. Remove the cardboard and observe what happens. Record your observations in Table 51-1.
8. Empty the jars. Fill one jar with warm water. Add salt and some food coloring.
9. Half fill the liter beaker with warm water.
10. Pour the salt water slowly down the side of the beaker into the fresh water.
11. Draw a diagram in Table 51-1 showing what happened and where the salt water collected.

Data and Observations
Table 51-1

Observations, Step 4: _____	Diagram:
Step 7: _____	

129

Questions and Conclusions

1. When you placed the cold water on top of the hot water, did currents form? _____
   Explain. _____
   _____

2. When you placed the hot water on top of the cold water, did currents form? _____
   Explain. _____

3. Which water is more dense, hot or cold? _____ How do you know? _____
   _____

4. Did the salt water mix with the fresh water? _____ Defend your answer.
   _____
   _____
   _____

5. Did the salt water collect in one place in the beaker? _____ Why? _____
   _____
   _____

6. Where is cold, dense water located in the ocean? _____
   _____
   Where is warm, less dense water located? _____
   _____

Strategy Check

_____ Can you determine the effect of temperature on the density of water?

_____ Can you determine the effect of dissolved slat on the density of water?

_____ Can you set a density current in motion?

_____ Can you explain density currents in the ocean?

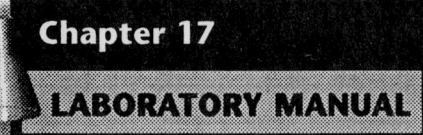

Chapter 17
LABORATORY MANUAL
Floating in Fresh Water and in Ocean Water 52

Fresh water and ocean water (salt water) have several different physical and chemical properties. One of the properties in which they differ influences how well an object floats. Both fresh water and salt water exert a buoyant force on a floating object.

Strategy
You will compare a boat floating in fresh water to a boat floating in salt water.
You will determine the relationship between the density of a liquid and its buoyant force.
You will observe how salt water and fresh water mix.

Materials
aluminum foil, 10 cm x 10 cm
balance
beaker (50 mL)
dropper
food coloring
water

grease pencil
metric ruler
ocean water (salt water—make solution with salt and water)
pencils (colored)
2 plastic storage boxes (clear)

Procedure
1. Fold the square of aluminum foil into a boat as shown below.

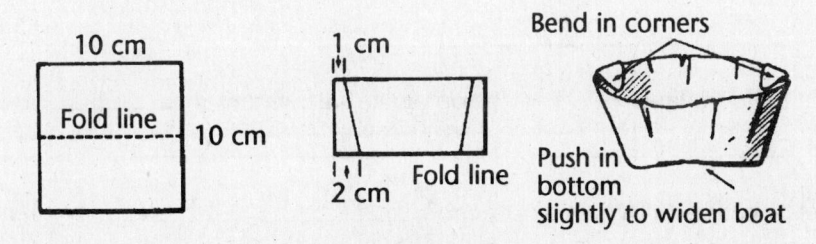

FIGURE 52-1

2. Pour 25 mL of salt water into a beaker. Determine the mass of the salt water. Record the volume and mass in Table 52-1.

3. Determine the mass of 25 mL of fresh water and record its volume and mass.

4. Half fill one plastic box with salt water. Half fill the other plastic box with fresh water.

5. Float the aluminum boat in the salt water. Mark the waterline on the boat using the grease pencil. Measure the distance from the bottom of the boat to the waterline. Record.

6. Float the same aluminum boat in the fresh water. Mark the waterline again.

7. Measure from the bottom of the boat to the new waterline and record.

8. Color the salt water using food coloring. Pour 25 mL of salt water into the beaker.

9. Using the dropper, add fresh water to the beaker until you see a layer of fresh water on top of the salt water. NOTE: Allow the fresh water to run slowly down the inside wall of the beaker so it does not disturb the salt water. Sketch the layers in the beaker in Table 52-1.

10. Allow the beaker to stand undisturbed for several days, then observe the results. Sketch the results in Table 52-1.

Data and Observations

Table 52-1

	Mass (g)	Volume (cm³)	Depth of waterline (cm)
Salt water			
Fresh water			
Beaker (start)		Beaker (after several days)	

Questions and Conclusions

1. In which liquid does the boat float higher? _____

2. State a hypothesis to explain this observation. _____
   _____

3. Defend your hypothesis with figures. _____
   _____

4. State the relationship between the density of a liquid and its buoyant force. _____
   _____

5. Why are you able to add a layer of water on top of the salt water? _____
   _____

6. Does this confirm or contradict your hypothesis? _____ Explain. _____
   _____

7. What can happen to two liquids with different densities if they are in contact over a long period of time? _____
   _____

8. What happens to the water in rivers when the river water flows into the ocean? _____
   _____

Strategy Check

____ Can you compare a boat floating in fresh water to a boat floating in salt water?

____ Can you determine the relationship between the density of a liquid and its buoyant force?

____ Can you observe how salt water and fresh water mix?

Chapter 18
LABORATORY MANUAL

Mapping the Ocean Floor 53

Mapping an ocean or lake floor is much different from mapping a continent. Scientists can't observe and measure underwater the same way they do on land. One way people can tell how deep water is is by lowering a weighted rope or chain. When the bottom of the rope or chain hits the ocean or lake floor, the rope or chain will become slack. By measuring how much of the rope or chain is in the water, a person can tell how deep the water is at that spot.

Strategy
You will make a model of the ocean floor, including all the major surface features.
You will make a map of a classmate's model.

Materials
large cardboard box with lid (box should be 22–30 cm deep and 30–45 cm long; dark paper can be used instead of lid as a cover)
cardboard tubes of various sizes (should be at least 15 cm long)
string with weight at one end or small chain (should be at least 12 inches longer than depth of box)
knife or scissors   masking tape   modeling clay
pen or pencil   ruler

Procedure
1. Work with a partner to prepare a model of the ocean floor. First, choose what features you will show. Be sure to include a continental shelf, continental slope, abyssal plain, and mid-ocean ridge. Then use cardboard tubes, modeling clay, and masking tape to form the features of your model along the bottom of the box. Be sure each ocean feature runs from side to side in the box. (See Figure 53-1.)

2. After you finish making your model, cut a 1 cm slit in the center of the lid, down its full length. Write your name on the box.

3. Exchange boxes with another classmate. Use your weighted string or chain to "map the ocean floor." At every 1 cm interval along the slit, lower your string or chain. When it hits the bottom of the "floor," pinch the string or chain gently even with the slit. Keeping your fingers in the same position, pull the string or chain out of the box and measure how deep the string or chain went before touching the bottom. Subtract this number from the height of the box. This will give you the depth of the ocean floor at this spot. Record your data in Table 53-1.

4. After completing your map, open the box and check your work. How accurate were you in mapping the ocean floor?

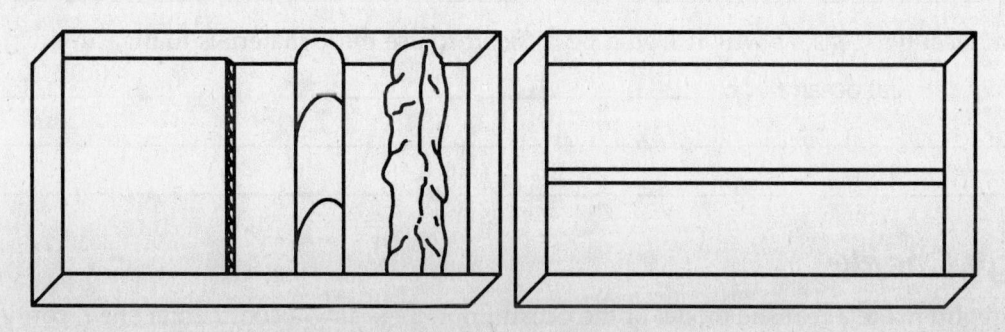

FIGURE 53-1

Data and Observations

Table 53-1 Ocean Floor

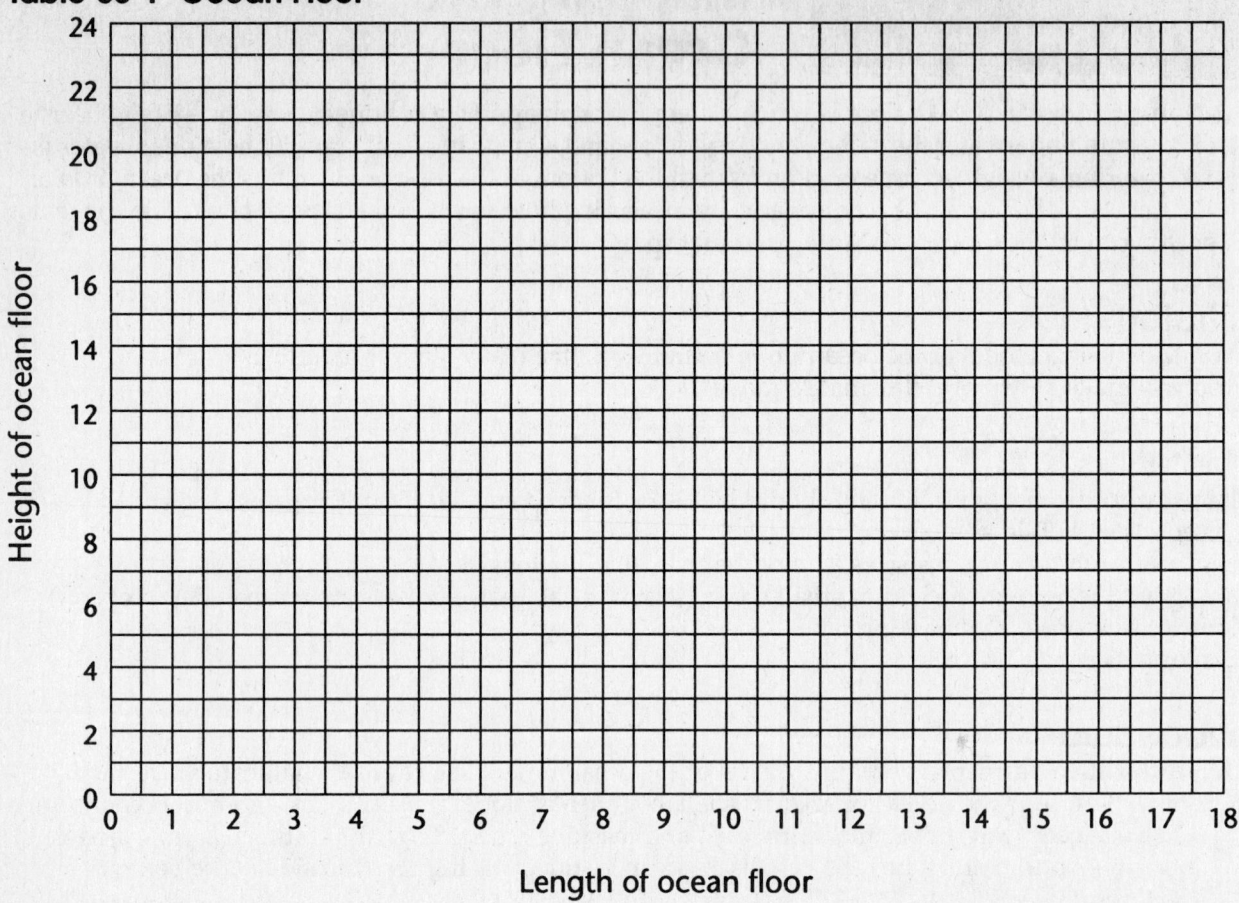

[Grid graph with x-axis "Length of ocean floor" (0-18) and y-axis "Height of ocean floor" (0-24)]

Questions and Conclusions

1. How accurate was your map? _____
_____

2. If readings were taken closer together, how would this affect the accuracy of your map? _____
_____

3. Some error is probably brought about by using a string or chain to measure the ocean depth. How could you improve these readings while still using the same equipment? _____
_____
_____

4. Give at least two reasons why it would be difficult to use these materials to measure distances for a map of the real ocean floor. _____
_____
_____

Strategy Check

_____ Can you make a realistic model of the ocean floor, including a continental shelf, continental slope, abyssal plain, and mid-ocean ridge?

_____ Can you fairly accurately map a model of the ocean floor?

Chapter 19
LABORATORY MANUAL
Human Impact on the Environment 54

Human beings are agents of change, and the rate at which they are changing the environment increases rapidly as population increases. Only recently have people become aware of their impact on the atmosphere, water, and the crust of Earth.

Strategy
You will make a survey of your neighborhood or town to observe people's impact on the environment.
You will use the accompanying matrix to estimate the ways in which humans have affected your local environment.
You will suggest some ways people can change their impact on the environment.

Materials
clipboard
environmental impact check sheet, Table 54-1
pencil

Procedure
1. Look over the check sheet on pages 136–137. A, B, C, and D are general categories for the way people change the environment. Across the top are the various areas of the environment that may be affected by the processes and materials that people use.

2. Walk through your neighborhood (in the city, at least a 10-block square) taking the sheet with you.

3. Place a check after each type of environmental influence found in your neighborhood. For example, if new houses are being built, put a check after "houses" in category A.

4. In the boxes to the right, put a diagonal slash under the area(s) affected by this influence. If the effect is good, put a plus in the lower right part of the box. If you think the effect is bad, place a minus in this position.

5. In the upper left of the box, place a number from 1 to 10 to indicate how much impact you think the change has or will have. If you think the change is small, write in 1; if you think it is or will be very large, write in 10. Use your judgment and observations to assign numbers 2 through 9 on this impact scale.

6. Find your total for each influence and for each affected area. Record your totals in the chart.

7. Find the class total for each influence and for each affected area. Record those totals in the chart.

Data and Observations

Table 54-1 Environmental Impact Check Sheet

	Biological	Scenic	Recreation	Temperature	Air	Water	Eutrophi-cation	Other	Totals
A. Construction—									
(Example) ✔		2 / +				3 / −	1 / −		2 / −
Houses									
Roads									
Transmission lines									
Fences or other barriers									
Canals									
Dams									
Shore structures									
Cut and fill									
Tunnels									
Mines									
Industrial plants									
Landscaped lawns									
B. Traffic—									
On roads									
Pipelines									
C. Chemicals—									
Fertilization									
Weed and insect control									
Deicing highways									
D. Waste disposal—									
Litter and dumps									

NAME _____ DATE _____ CLASS _____

	Biological	Scenic	Recreation	Temperature	Air	Water	Eutrophication	Other	Totals
Sewage									
Stack and exhaust emissions									
Cooling water discharge									
Used-lubricant dumping									
Totals									
Class Totals									

Questions and Conclusions

1. List three ways in which the construction of concrete pavement (roads) changes the environment.
   _____
   _____

2. How does an automobile affect the atmosphere? _____

3. What other ways could people use to travel that would have less adverse effects on the environment? _____
   _____
   _____

4. If there is smog in your local area, what is its source? _____
   _____

5. What can be done to reduce or eliminate the smog? _____
   _____
   _____

6. What resources are being used in local construction? _____
   _____
   _____

7. What resources are lost to humans when cities move into the surrounding countryside? _____

8. Are there alternatives? _____

9. Discuss the drawbacks of the alternatives you have listed in the questions above. _____

Strategy Check

____ Can you recognize human influence on your local environment?

____ Can you estimate the impact, good or bad, using the matrix?

____ Can you suggest and evaluate alternatives?

NAME _____ DATE _____ CLASS _____

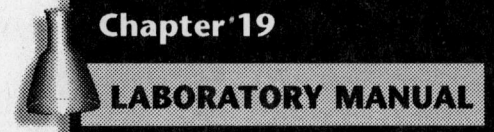

Chapter 19
LABORATORY MANUAL

Reclamation of Mine Wastes 55

Mine wastes, which seem to be worthless, can be made profitable. For example, copper metal can be reclaimed from copper mine waste. When open pit copper is crushed and smelted, copper (II) sulfate is left in the waste rock. The copper (II) sulfate can be dissolved in water. Then more metallic copper can be removed by reacting the copper (II) sulfate with iron ores.

Strategy
You will investigate a process by which copper is reclaimed from open pit waste.

Materials
apron
balance
beaker (500 mL)
copper (II) sulfate crystals, $CuSO_4$
goggles
graduated cylinder (50 mL)
litmus paper (blue)
nails (iron scraps)
water

Procedure
1. Place 3 grams of copper (II) sulfate in the beaker. **CAUTION:** *Copper (II) sulfate is poisonous. Avoid contact with skin.*

2. Cover the copper (II) sulfate crystals with 50 mL of water. Record the color of the solution in Table 55-1. Test with litmus; record your results in Table 55-1.

3. Place the iron scrap in the solution. Observe and record what happens in Table 55-1.

4. Test the solution with blue litmus paper and record your results in Table 55-1.

Data and Observations

Table 55-1

Solution	Color	Litmus	Other observations
Copper(II) sulfate			
Copper(II) sulfate and iron			

Questions and Conclusions

1. Why did you add water to the copper (II) sulfate crystals? _____

2. What happens to the copper in the solution when iron is added? _____

3. Is this a chemical or physical method of reclaiming the copper? _____

4. What happened to the water in which the copper (II) sulfate is dissolved? _____
   _____

5. Does this method use up all the waste material? _____

6. What might happen to a stream if large amounts of the water used in this reclaiming process were flushed into it? _____
   _____
   _____

7. What might happen to an abandoned copper mine in a humid climate? _____
   _____
   _____

Strategy Check

_____ Can you recognize the copper deposit on the iron?

_____ Could copper be reclaimed from waste using this method?

_____ Would reclaiming the copper be profitable?

NAME _____ DATE _____ CLASS _____

Chapter 19
LABORATORY MANUAL • Conservation—Recycling 56

You can do little about some changes in our environment. One thing, however, that you can do is to avoid waste. As we begin to understand the limitations of our resources, we are finding ways to conserve some materials.

Strategy
You will work with your class to collect some waste materials.
You will find out what companies reuse such materials.
You will interview a representative of a company and learn how that company recycles or conserves materials.

Materials
4 baby food jars   poster paint
brush, soft   water
poster board

Procedure
1. Look in the phone book to find out who in your vicinity will accept materials for recycling projects. If there is no recycling project in your area, start your own.

2. Make a poster to tell the public that your group will collect material for recycling. It should be large enough to be placed in a business or store window.

3. Survey your neighborhood and promote the collecting project.

4. At home keep a special container for glass and one for aluminum. These materials now are being recycled. Flatten the aluminum cans to save space. Once a week deliver these containers to a collection center.

5. Keep a list of the kinds of waste in your own home in Table 56-1. Check what type of waste it is.

6. Select a company in your area. Interview a representative of the company. Find out what raw materials the company uses, what wastes are produced, and what the company does with the wastes. Write a summary of the interview.

Data and Observations (See page 142.)

Questions and Conclusions
1. What materials are saved when glass is reused? _____

2. If glass is recycled for use in pavement, what is another advantage, in addition to saving glass? _____

3. What are the most common waste items in homes? _____
   Which of these is (are) biodegradable? _____

4. Why are rubber tires so difficult to get rid of as waste? _____

5. Which waste items are being recycled now? _____
_____

Which items could be recycled? _____
_____

6. Why are we not recycling more wastes? _____
_____

7. How are companies in your area practicing conservation and recycling? _____
_____

Data and Observations

Table 56-1

Waste	Biodegradable (breaks down naturally)	Metal	Nonmetal	Synthetic

Strategy Check

____ Can you collect waste materials?

____ Can you find companies that reuse materials?

____ Can you find out what a company is doing to practice conservation and recycling?

NAME	DATE	CLASS

Chapter 20
LABORATORY MANUAL
Smoke Pollution 57

The U.S. Bureau of Mines has adopted the Ringelmann Chart as its basic scale for measuring smoke pollution. Using an adapted version of this chart, you can recognize which smokestacks may be polluting your environment.

Strategy
You will observe an industry that is sending out smoke.
You will keep track of this industry for a week to see whether its smoke is a one-time emission or a constant practice.

Materials
cardboard (thin)   glue or paste   scissors
compass   Ringelmann Chart, Figure 57-1

Procedure
1. Cut out Figure 57-1 and glue it to the cardboard.
2. When the glue is dry, cut out the center window by cutting along the dotted lines.
3. Go outside and observe a source of industrial smoke.
4. View the smoke through the window while holding the chart at arm's length.
5. Match the color of the darkest part of the smoke plume to one of the examples on the chart.
6. Continue observing the smoke plume for about five minutes. Record the name of the company emitting the smoke, the wind direction, wind speed, time of day, and the number of the matching smoke column in Table 57-1.
7. If there are many stacks in the area, determine which stack is emitting the darkest smoke.
8. Repeat these observations every day for a week. Make your readings the same time each day.

Data and Observations (See page 144.)

Questions and Conclusions
1. If accidental air pollution occurred, what kinds of readings would you expect? _____
   _____

2. What does Number 5 on the Ringelmann Chart indicate about the relative amount of pollution entering the atmosphere? _____
   _____

3. What effect does wind have on pollution in your local area? _____
   _____
   _____

4. List the companies that appear to add the most pollutants to your local atmosphere.
   _____
   _____

5. What processes are involved in these industries? _____
_____
_____

6. How might they reduce the pollution? _____
_____

7. Some companies emit invisible gases. Might these gases also be pollutants? Explain. _____
_____
_____
_____

Data and Observations

Table 57-1

Day	Wind direction (north, south, southeast)	Wind speed (light, strong, gusty)	Time of day	Darkness of smoke (from chart)	Company's name
1					
2					
3					
4					
5					

Strategy Check

_____ Can you tell which smokestacks are giving off the darkest smoke?

_____ Can you see how wind influences smoke?

_____ Can you tell, after a week of viewing, if the industry is constantly giving off large amounts of smoke?

NAME	DATE	CLASS

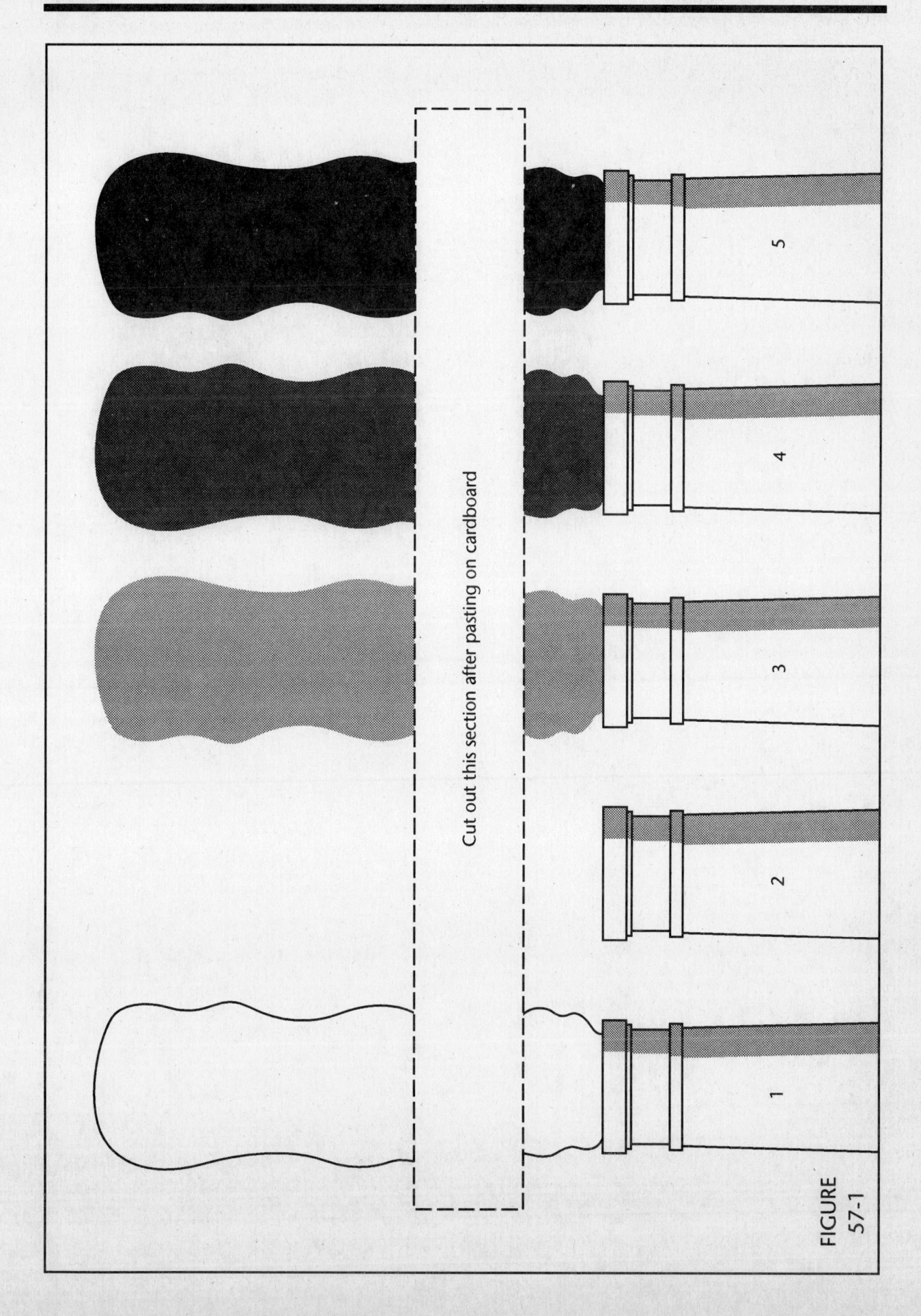

Cut out this section after pasting on cardboard

1
2
3
4
5

FIGURE 57-1

Chapter 20

LABORATORY MANUAL

Water Purification 58

Pure water is essential to all life forms. But what about a situation in which you do not have pure water available? Life rafts on boats are equipped with an apparatus that can be used to distill water from salt water. Desert safety survival rules provide another means to distill water.

Strategy
You will purify water by using a simple distillation process.
You will discuss how this process could be used in an emergency situation.

Materials
cereal bowl
2 coat hangers, or bendable wire
pan (larger than the circumference of the bag)
pen (felt-tip)
plastic bag (clear)
sand (fine) or soil
sunlamp or bright sunshine
water

Procedure
1. Bend the coat hangers into a frame; see Figure 58-1.
2. Mix the sand or soil into water in the cereal bowl. Mark the water level on the inside with the pen.
3. Place the cereal bowl in the pan and place the wire frame over it.
4. Pull the plastic bag over the frame until it touches the pan. Record the appearance of the water.
5. Set the apparatus in direct sun or under a sunlamp.
6. Allow the apparatus to stand undisturbed. Observe and record your observations after about 10 minutes and again after 30 minutes in Table 58-1.

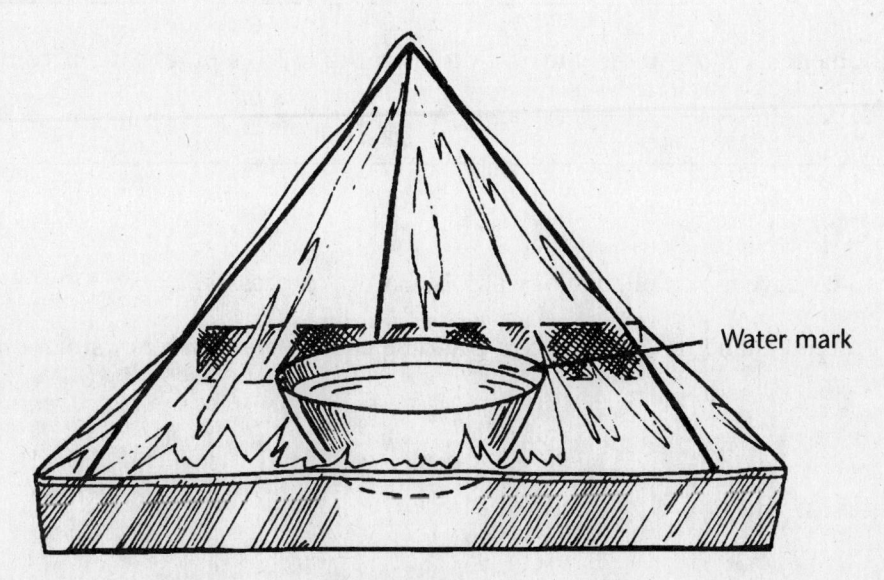

FIGURE 58-1

Data and Observations

Table 58-1

Time (min)	Observations
0	Water color _____ Inside of plastic bag _____
10	Water level _____ Inside of plastic bag _____
30	Water level _____ Inside of plastic bag _____

Questions and Conclusions

1. What happened to the water level in the cereal bowl? _____

2. Why did water form on the inside of the plastic bag? _____
   _____

3. What two processes are involved in this activity? _____
   Identify the energy source. _____

4. How could you prove that the water that forms on the inside of the plastic bag is pure? ____
   _____
   _____

5. What equipment should you carry in a vehicle in order to have pure water if you are going to cross a desert? _____
   _____

Strategy Check

_____ Can you observe the distillation of water by natural processes?

_____ Can you understand how this process could be used in an emergency situation?

NAME _____ DATE _____ CLASS _____

Chapter 21
LABORATORY MANUAL
Refraction of Light 59

When light from a star reaches Earth, the light is refracted, or bent, as it enters the atmosphere. The refraction of light waves is caused by an increase or decrease in the speed of light. As light passes from one transparent substance to another, its speed changes. Refraction changes the direction of the light waves. Therefore, we see most stars in positions that appear higher in the sky than they actually are. The closer the star is to its high point or zenith, the closer its apparent position is to its true position.

To be refracted, light must strike the surface of a transparent material at an angle. The speed of light in air is very close to the speed of light in a vacuum. Therefore, the index of refraction is usually found by comparing the speed of light in air and in another substance.

Strategy
You will diagram the refraction of light waves.
You will plot the true position of a star based on the refraction of light.

Materials
beaker (100 mL)   plastic drinking glass (clear)   pencil
coin   pan (shallow)   water

Procedure
1. Place the pencil in the empty glass and observe the pencil through the side of the glass. Draw a diagram showing your observations in Table 59-1.

2. Add water to just below the rim of the glass. View the pencil again. Draw a diagram showing your observations in Table 59-1.

3. Place a coin in the pan in a position where you cannot see it over the top of the pan. Diagram this position. Add water to the pan until you can see the coin without changing your position. Sketch your diagrams in Table 59-1.

Data and Observations
Table 59-1

Pencil	Coin
Air	Air
Water	Water

Copyright © Glencoe/McGraw-Hill, a division of The McGraw-Hill Companies, Inc.

149

Questions and Conclusions

1. Why does the pencil appear to bend in water? _____
   _____

2. Why does the coin come into view when water is added to the pan? _____
   _____

3. What causes light from the stars to be refracted? _____
   _____

   Why is this refracting greatest at the horizon? _____
   _____

4. The velocity of light changes as it passes from air to water. What happens to the velocity of light when it passes from a vacuum (or near vacuum) into air? _____
   _____
   _____

5. How do you see sunlight after the sun is below the horizon? _____
   _____
   _____

6. Look at the diagram below. The star is shown in its actual positions at zenith and at the horizon. Diagram its observed positions in both cases.

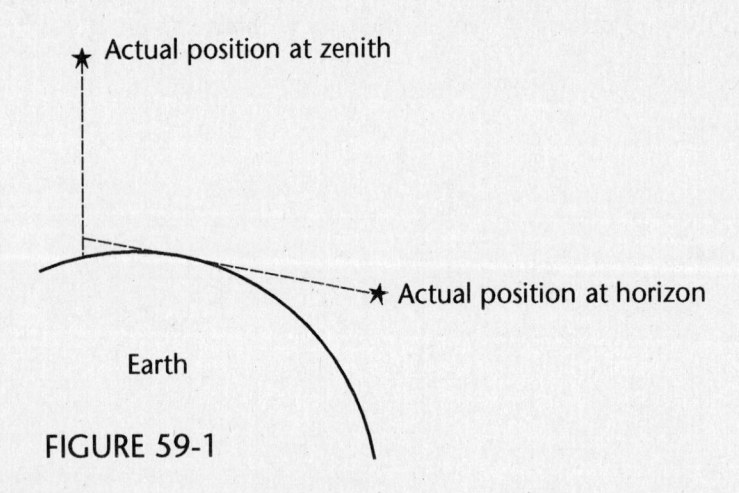

★ Actual position at zenith

★ Actual position at horizon

Earth

FIGURE 59-1

Strategy Check

_____ Can you observe the refraction of light waves?

_____ Can you plot the true position of a star based on refraction of light?

NAME _____ DATE _____ CLASS _____

Chapter 21
LABORATORY MANUAL
• Spectral Analysis 60

The photograph of the spectrum of a star, sorted by color across a plate, will reveal spectral lines upon close examination. The lines are produced by elements in a star at high temperature. These lines represent the chemical composition of the star. Each element has its own "fingerprint." To analyze the spectra of stars, scientists collected spectra of all the known elements. If we compare the spectral lines of an unknown star with the spectral lines of elements, we can determine the chemical composition of the star. More recently, we have discovered not only the composition of the stars but also their temperatures, their rotational rate, and their relative motion with regard to Earth.

Strategy
You will construct a simple spectral analyzer.
You will determine the composition of a star using the spectral analyzer.
You will determine other characteristics of a star by comparing the spectral lines with a standard.

Materials
page 153 of this book
scissors

Procedure
1. Cut out pull tab card found on page 153, spectroscope fingerprints card, and Stars B, C, and D along the dashed lines.
2. Make 5 slits along the dashed lines A, B, C, D, and E on the fingerprints card.
3. From left to right, insert "Pull Tab Out" up through slit E, down through slit D, up through slit C, down through slit B, and up through slit A.
4. Keeping the sodium doublets aligned, compare the lines of each known element with the lines of Star A. If lines match, then that element is present in Star A. Record your findings in Table 60-1.
5. Star B, Star C, and Star D are provided for further study and comparison. Each can be placed over Star A.

Data and Observations
Table 60-1

Star	A Chemical Composition	B Other Characteristics
A		
B		
C		
D		

Questions and Conclusions

1. When we say that the neon colored lights look beautiful at night, what color comes to mind? _____ What color is suggested by the "fingerprints" of neon? _____
_____

2. Did any of the stars have the same chemical composition? Look at column A of the Table.
_____
_____
_____

3. Sometimes scientists see spectral lines that do not fit the usual pattern. The lines might be shifted from their usual positions. This may suggest that the star is moving either toward the observer (shift toward the blue) or moving away from the observer (shift toward the red). Look at the spectral lines for Star B and Star D. Star B is the standard for comparison. How is Star D different? What is a possible explanation for the difference? _____
_____
_____

4. If the scientist sees the spectral lines wider than usual, he or she relates this spectral broadening to either rotational speed (the broader the faster), temperature (the broader the hotter), or pressure (the broader the greater pressure). Look at the spectral lines for Star B and Star C. Star B is the standard. How is Star C different? What could be a possible explanation? _____
_____
_____

5. Fill out column B in Table 60-1.

Strategy Check

_____ Can you construct a simple spectral analyzer?

_____ Can you determine the composition of a star using the spectral analyzer?

_____ Can you determine other characteristics of a star by comparing the spectral lines with a standard?

NAME _____ DATE _____ CLASS _____

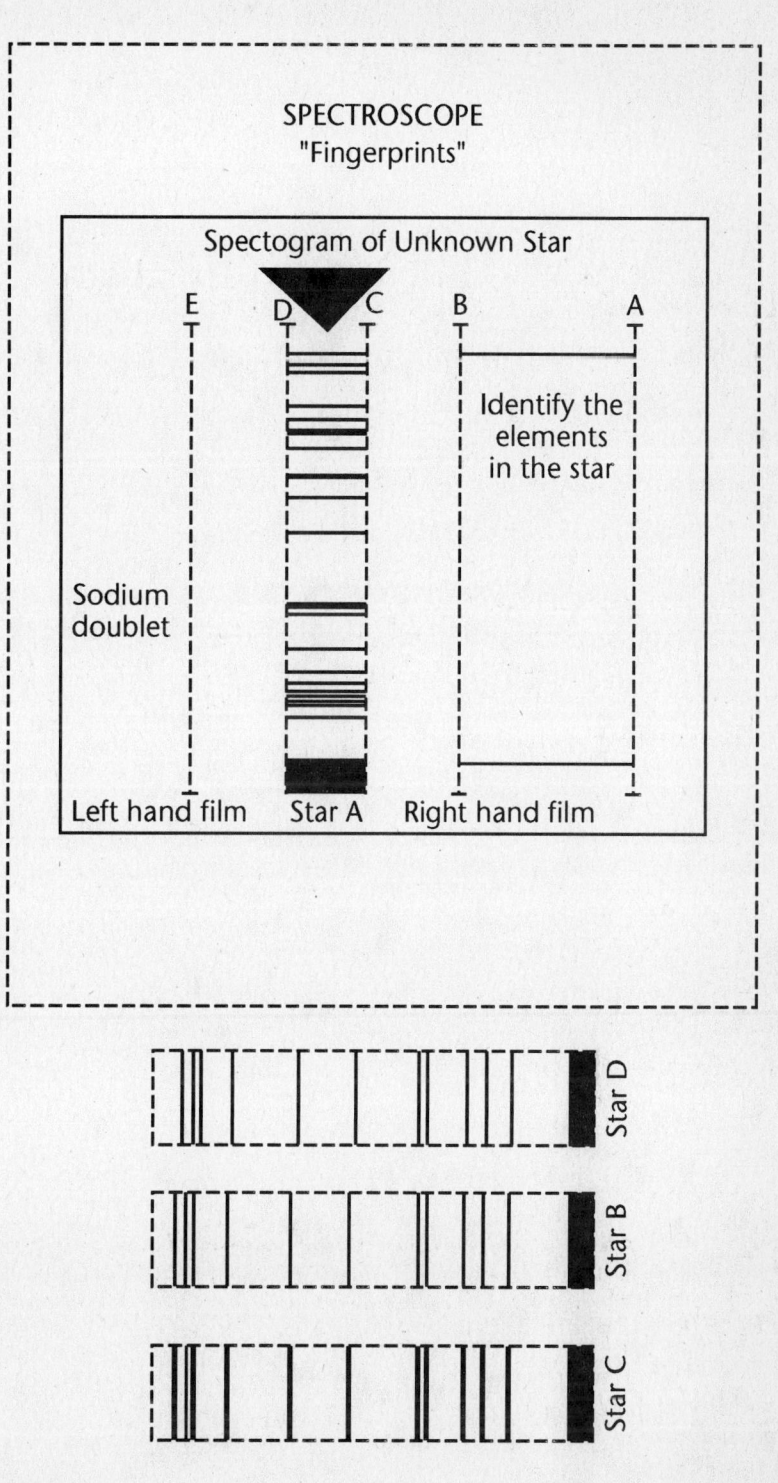

Pull Tab Out

| Indigo | Blue | Green | Yellow | Red |

Neon

Mercury

Argon

Helium

Hydrogen

Sodium

Calcium

Iron

4000 Å   5000 Å   6000 Å   7000 Å

SPECTROSCOPE
"Fingerprints"

Spectogram of Unknown Star

E   D   C   B   A

Identify the elements in the star

Sodium doublet

Left hand film — Star A — Right hand film

Star D

Star B

Star C

Copyright © Glencoe/McGraw-Hill, a division of the McGraw-Hill Companies, Inc.

Chapter 22
LABORATORY MANUAL

• Earth's Spin 61

The speed at which Earth turns on its axis can be described in two ways. The velocity of rotation refers to the rate at which Earth turns on its axis. Velocity of rotation refers to Earth as a whole. For any point on Earth's surface, the speed of Earth's rotation can be described as its instantaneous linear velocity. This velocity is the speed of the point as it follows a circular path around Earth.

Strategy
You will determine the instantaneous linear velocity of some points on Earth.
You will compare the linear velocities of points at different locations on Earth.

Materials
globe (mounted on axis)   stopwatch   tape (adhesive)
meterstick   string

Procedure
Part A

1. Place small pieces of adhesive tape on the Prime Meridian, at the equator, at 30° N latitude, at 60° N latitude, and at the north pole.

2. Line up the tape with the metal circle above the globe; see Figure 61-1.

3. With your finger on the globe, move it west to east for one second; see Figure 61-2.

4. For each location marked by tape, measure the distance from the Prime Meridian to the metal circle. Use the string and the meterstick to get accurate distances. Record the distances in Table 61-1.

5. Realign the metal circle with the pieces of tape. Move the globe west to east for two seconds. Record the distances from the tapes to the metal circle in Table 61-1.

6. Repeat Step 5, moving the globe for three seconds. Record your results in Table 61-1.

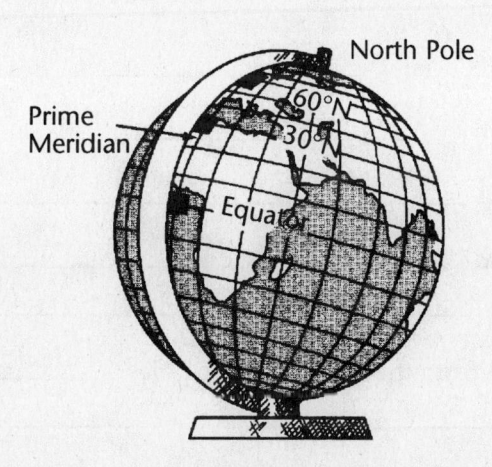

FIGURE 61-1

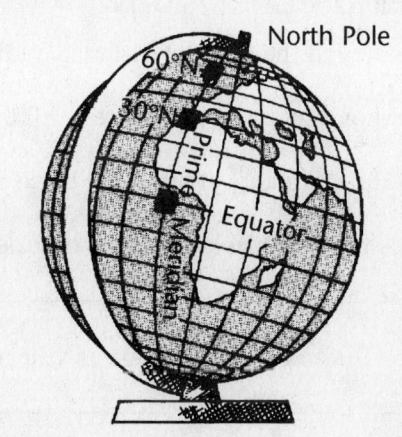

FIGURE 61-2

Part B

Calculate the speed of each point for each trial. Record in Table 61-2. Use the formula:

velocity (cm/s) = $\dfrac{distance\ (cm)}{time\ (s)}$

Data and Observations

Table 61-1

Latitude	Distance moved (cm)		
	1 s	2 s	3 s
Equator			
30° N			
60° N			
North Pole			

Table 61-2

Latitude	Velocity (cm/s)		
	Trial 1	Trial 2	Trial 3
Equator			
30° N			
60° N			
North Pole			

Questions and Conclusions

1. Which point moved the farthest distance in all three trials? _____

2. Which point moved the least distance in all three trials? _____

3. Which point did not move at all in the three trials? _____

4. On what does the linear velocity of a point depend? _____

5. How does the linear velocity change as you move from the equator to the poles? _____

Strategy Check

_____ Can you determine instantaneous linear velocity?

_____ Can you see that the linear velocity is not the same for all points on Earth?

Chapter 22
LABORATORY MANUAL
Earth's Magnetism 62

The physical force of magnetism is one of the observable properties of Earth. Earth is similar to a bar magnet in the way it behaves. The positive end of Earth's magnetic pole is near the north geographic pole. The negative end of the magnetic pole is near the south geographic pole.

When rocks containing iron minerals harden, their molecules tend to line up pointing toward the north magnetic pole. Studies of rocks containing such minerals indicate that the continents have wandered from place to place. Scientists assume that the magnetic pole always has been within 15° of the geographic pole. Rocks suggesting a different location for the magnetic pole provide a clue to the former location of the continent.

Strategy
You will use a compass.
You will map the magnetic field in your classroom.

Materials
compass
graph paper

Procedure
1. Draw a floor plan of the classroom on the graph paper. (The floor plan does not have to be to scale.) Indicate north, south, east, and west on the floor plan.

2. Mark the desk locations on the floor plan with a small circle and a number.

3. Take a compass reading at each numbered location. Note the compass needle's direction (see Figure 62-1) and draw it neatly on the floor plan. Record each angle in Table 62-1.

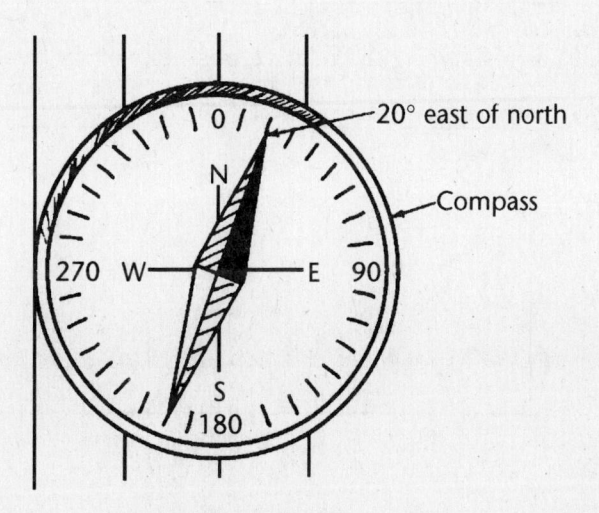

FIGURE 62-1

Data and Observations

Table 62-1

Location	Angle
1	
2	
3	
4	
5	
6	
7	

Questions and Conclusions

1. In what direction did your compass needle point in most of the readings? _____

2. Why isn't magnetic north the same as geographic north? _____
   _____
   _____
   _____

3. Are any of the compass readings markedly different? _____ Why?
   _____

4. Draw a diagram of Earth showing the relative positions of the geographic axis and the magnetic axis.

Strategy Check

_____ Can you use a compass?

_____ Can you make a magnetic map of your classroom?

Chapter 22
LABORATORY MANUAL
Moon Phases 63

The moon, like Earth, shines by reflecting light from the sun. Because the moon revolves around Earth, its reflected light is not always visible from Earth. When Earth is between the sun and the moon, half of the moon is illuminated (lighted). This is the full moon phase. When the moon is between the sun and Earth, we cannot see the lighted side of the moon. This is the new moon phase. Following the new moon, we see a slender crescent, then a quarter moon, then a gibbous (more than a quarter) moon, and finally the full moon. After full moon, the phases reverse until the moon is invisible again. Because the moon's period of rotation is about the same as its period of revolution around Earth, we always see the same side of the moon. The complete lunar phase cycle takes about 29 1/4 days—new moon to new moon. This is also called a synodic month.

Strategy
You will demonstrate the phases of the moon.

Materials
flashlight, lamp, or slide projector light
globe
plastic foam ball (1/4 size of globe)
30 cm wire (stiff)

Procedure
1. Push the wire through the plastic foam ball (moon), and make a right angle bend in the wire at about 15 cm.
2. Place the globe (Earth) on a desk so you can walk completely around it.
3. Place the lamp, flashlight, or projector light (sun) about two meters from Earth.
4. Place the moon between Earth and the sun. Hold the moon's axis at about an 84° angle from the plane of its orbit.
5. Observe the moon from Earth. Record your observations of the moon on Figure 63-1 at position *a*. Then move the moon 1/4 of the way around Earth in a counterclockwise direction. Record your observations on Figure 63-1 at position *b*. Do the same with the moon 1/2 of the way around Earth (position *c* on Figure 63-1) and 3/4 of the way around Earth (position *d* on Figure 63-1).
6. Place the moon again between Earth and the sun.
7. Observe Earth and the moon from "space" (a position directly above Earth). Record your observations of the moon on Figure 63-2 at position *a*.
8. Again move the moon 1/4 of the way around Earth in a counterclockwise direction. Record your observations of the moon on Figure 63-2 at position *b*. Do the same with the moon 1/2 of the way around Earth (position *c* on Figure 63-2) and 3/4 of the way around Earth (position *d* on Figure 63-2).

Data and Observations

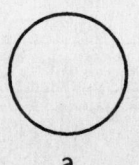

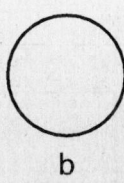

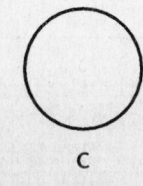

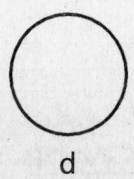

○ ○ ○ ○
a   b   c   d

FIGURE 63-1

FIGURE 63-2

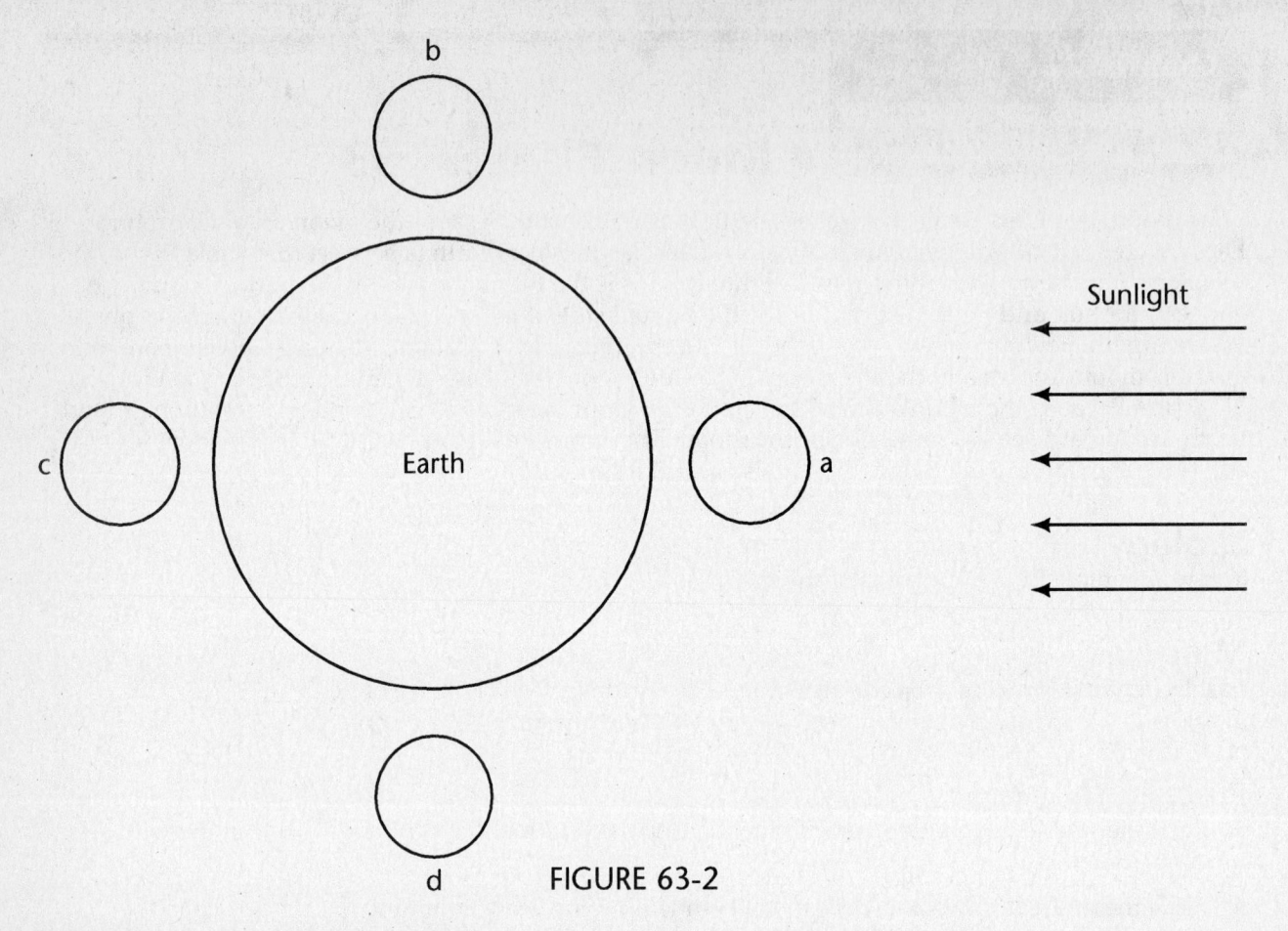

Questions and Conclusions

1. What is the phase called when you cannot see the moon from Earth? _____
   _____

2. Why is position *b* in both figures called first quarter moon? _____
   _____

   When the moon is in this position, how much of it can you see from Earth? _____
   _____

3. Why is position *c* called full moon? _____
   _____

4. At what moon phase is a lunar eclipse possible? _____

5. How often would a lunar eclipse occur if the moon's orbit were not tilted? _____
   _____

   Why? _____
   _____

Strategy Check

_____ Can you demonstrate the phases of the moon?

NAME _____ DATE _____ CLASS _____

Chapter 22
LABORATORY MANUAL
• Newton's First Law of Motion 64

One of Isaac Newton's laws of motion states that all bodies at rest resist motion. However, once a body is set in motion by an outside force, the body moves in a straight line until another force stops it or causes it to change direction. The force that stops or deflects the body may be air pressure, friction, or another body.

Strategy
You will measure the amount of force needed to set a body in motion.
You will deduce the relationship between the force needed to start a body in motion and the mass of the body.

Materials
balance   spring scale
bricks

Procedure
1. Determine the mass of one brick. Record in Table 64-1.
2. Attach the brick to the spring scale. Pull the brick slowly across the floor.
3. Record the force needed to start the brick in motion. Record the force needed to keep the brick in motion.
4. Determine the mass of the second brick. Add the mass to the mass of the first brick. Record in Table 64-1.
5. Repeat Steps 2 and 3.
6. Determine the mass of the third brick. Add the mass to the mass of the other bricks. Record in Table 64-1.
7. Repeat Steps 2 and 3.

Data and Observations
Table 64-1

Number of bricks	Mass (g)	Force (N) Start	Force (N) Keep in motion
1			
2			
3			

Questions and Conclusions

1. What is the outside force that starts the brick(s) in motion? _____

2. Compare the force needed to start the brick(s) in motion and the force needed to keep the brick(s) in motion. _____
_____
_____

3. Compare the force required to keep the brick(s) in motion to the mass of the brick(s). _____
_____
_____
_____

4. State the relationship between the force needed to start a body in motion and the body's mass.
_____
_____
_____

5. What force resists the motion of the bricks in all cases? _____

6. Explain in terms of Newtons' law of motion what happens to a passenger who is standing in the aisle of a bus when the bus stops suddenly. Use diagrams to help explain your answer.
_____
_____
_____

7. If the force of the sun's gravity suddenly stopped acting on the planets, in what kind of path would the planets move? _____

Strategy Check

____ Can you measure the amount of force needed to set a body in motion?

____ Can you state the relationship between the force needed to start a body in motion and the mass of the body?

NAME _____ DATE _____ CLASS _____

Chapter 23
LABORATORY MANUAL

Venus—The Greenhouse Effect 65

Because Venus is closer to the sun, it receives almost twice the amount of solar radiation received by Earth. Venus reflects more radiation to space than Earth because of its clouds. We might expect Venus, therefore, to have surface temperatures similar to Earth. However, the *Pioneer* Venus vehicles have measured surface temperatures of 460°C. Some scientists explain this high temperature as the "greenhouse effect." When the solar energy strikes the surface of Venus, the energy is absorbed and changed into heat energy. This heat energy is reflected back to the atmosphere where it is trapped.

Strategy

You will build a model to show the greenhouse effect.
You will compare this model to Earth.
You will form a hypothesis about temperatures on Venus using data collected from this model and from the *Pioneer* spacecraft.

Materials

cardboard (stiff)   pencils (colored)   thermometer
graph paper   plastic storage box and lid, clear   watch
heat lamp (mounted)   soil

Procedure

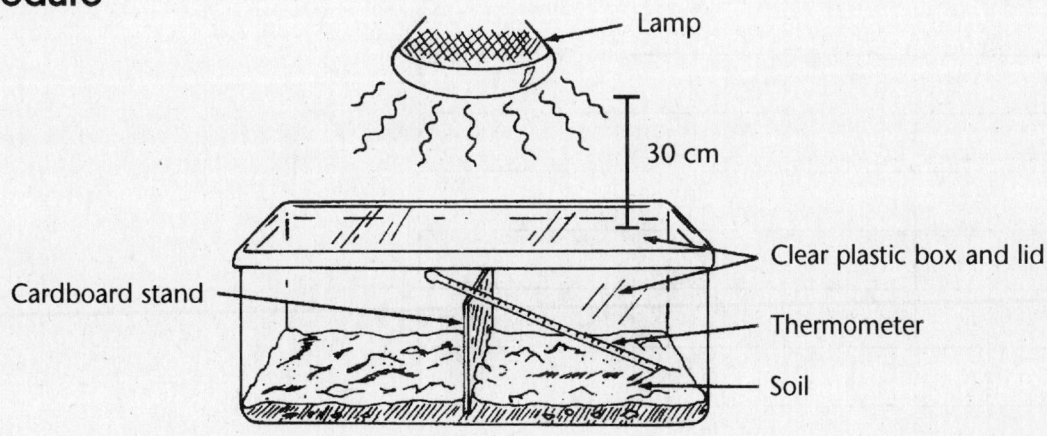

FIGURE 65-1

1. Place about 3 centimeters of soil in the bottom of the clear plastic box.

2. Thoroughly moisten the soil with water.

3. Cut the piece of cardboard so that it makes a divider for the box. The cardboard should not quite reach the top of the box. Insert the divider into the box.

4. Lean the thermometer against the divider with the bulb end up; see Figure 65-1. Put the lid on the box.

5. Position the box and lamp in an area of the room where no direct sunlight reaches.

6. Place the heat lamp about 30 centimeters above the box and direct the light so it shines on the thermometer bulb.

Copyright © Glencoe/McGraw-Hill, a division of The McGraw-Hill Companies, Inc.

7. Turn off the lamp and allow the thermometer to return to room temperature. Record room temperature in Table 65-1.

8. Turn on the lamp and measure the temperature every minute for 20 minutes. Record the temperatures in Table 65-1.

9. Turn off the lamp and allow the thermometer to return to room temperature. Remoisten the soil and repeat Step 8 with the lid off the box. Record your data in Table 65-1.

Data and Observations

Table 65-1

Time (min)	Temperature (°C) Lid off	Lid on
1		
2		
3		
4		
5		
6		
7		
8		
9		
10		
11		
12		
13		
14		
15		
16		
17		
18		
19		
20		

Graph the data using two different colors. Plot Temperature on the vertical axis and Time on the horizontal axis.

NAME _____ DATE _____ CLASS _____

Questions and Conclusions

1. Did the temperature increase the most with the lid on or off? _____
   Why? _____
   _____
   _____

2. Draw a diagram of Earth showing its atmosphere and what occurs to solar radiation in the atmosphere. List the components of Earth's atmosphere on your diagram. Write a brief explanation of the greenhouse effect on Earth. _____
   _____
   _____
   _____
   _____

3. Compare the activity to the greenhouse effect on Earth. How are they similar? How are they different? _____
   _____
   _____
   _____
   _____

4. Venus' atmosphere is composed mainly of carbon dioxide, carbon monoxide, water, nitrogen, and sulfuric acid. Venus' atmosphere is 100 times as dense as Earth's atmosphere. From the surface of Venus up to 20 km, there appears to be a clear region of atmosphere. A thick layer of clouds extends from about 50 km to 80 km above the surface of Venus. These clouds are composed of drops of sulfuric acid. Above and below these clouds are other thinner layers of haze. Venus' ionosphere extends from 100 km to 200 km above the surface. Like the ionosphere of Earth, it has layers. The temperature in the ionosphere of Venus is cooler than the temperature in Earth's ionosphere.

   Draw a diagram of Venus showing its atmosphere and what happens to solar radiation in the atmosphere. List the components of Venus' atmosphere on your diagram. Write a brief explanation of the greenhouse effect on Venus. _____
   _____
   _____
   _____

5. Compare the greenhouse effect on Earth and Venus. Can you think of a reason why the surface of Venus is so much hotter than the surface of Earth? _____
   _____
   _____
   _____

Strategy Check

_____ Can you build a model to show the greenhouse effect?

_____ Can you compare this model to Earth?

_____ Can you form a hypothesis about the surface temperature of Venus?

NAME _____ DATE _____ CLASS _____

Chapter 23
LABORATORY MANUAL

Jupiter and Its Moons 66

Jupiter and its moons are similar to a model of the solar system. Four of the moons are called the Galilean moons since Galileo first observed them in 1610. The moons are called Io, Ganymede, Callisto, and Europa.

Strategy
You will build an astronomical telescope.
You will observe the Galilean moons of Jupiter.
You will place the four moons in order outward from Jupiter.

Materials
2 cardboard mailing tubes, 9 cm and 18 cm (9-cm one should be slightly smaller in diameter than the 18-cm one)
2 convex lenses
    eyepiece, short focal length
    objective, long focal length
tape (masking)
Star and Sky, *Astronomy*, or *Sky and Telescope*, current issue

Procedure
1. Tape the objective lens to one end of the larger, longer tube.
2. Tape the eyepiece lens to one end of the smaller, shorter tube.
3. Slide the small tube inside the large tube.
4. View a book through the telescope. Move the small tube back and forth to focus. Record your observations under Data and Observations.
5. Look up the position of Jupiter in a current issue of one of the magazines.
6. After dark, take the telescope outside and locate Jupiter. Observe and sketch the four visible moons. Sketch the moons in Table 66-1.
7. Repeat this observation every clear night for two weeks. Record all data in Table 66-1.

Data and Observations
Observations of book using the telescope: _____
_____
_____
_____

Table 66-1

Date/Time	Moon	Sketch

Questions and Conclusions

1. Why is the book upside down when you view it through the telescope? _____
_____
_____

2. List the four Galilean moons of Jupiter in order outward from Jupiter. _____
_____

3. Write a brief description of each moon. Use magazines such as *Newsweek, Time, Science, Scientific American,* or *Astronomy* as sources for your material. _____
_____
_____
_____
_____

Strategy Check

____ Can you build an astronomical telescope?

____ Can you place Jupiter's moons in order outward from the planet?

NAME _____ DATE _____ CLASS _____

Chapter 24
LABORATORY MANUAL

Astronomical Distances 67

Astronomers must work with very large numbers in calculating distances in the universe. Light from our sun takes eight minutes to reach Earth. Light emitted by the next closest star, Proxima Centauri, takes 4.2 years. How far is Proxima Centauri? The distance light travels in one year is 9.5 trillion kilometers. This distance is called a light-year. The distance to Proxima Centauri is about 40 trillion kilometers. Can you imagine this distance?

Strategy
You will choose a scale to represent the distances in the solar system.
You will use this scale to visually illustrate the distances among the sun and the planets.

Materials
adding machine tape
meterstick
pen (felt-tip)

Procedure
1. Calculate a scale of distances to map the solar system. Record your scale and the distance from the sun to each planet in Table 67-1.
2. Place a dot at the end of the adding machine tape to represent the sun.
3. Place the planets in correct order on the tape from the sun.

Data and Observations *(See page 170.)*

Questions and Conclusions
1. What scale did you choose? _____ Why? _____
   _____

2. Using your scale, calculate how far Proxima Centauri would be from the sun. Proxima Centauri is about 40 trillion kilometers away. _____

3. A round trip to the moon requires about one week of Earth time. The moon is about 386 000 kilometers away. How long would it take to make a round trip to Proxima Centauri?
   _____

Strategy Check
_____ Can you choose a scale to represent distances in the solar system?

_____ Can you calculate these distances to another star?

Data and Observations

Table 67-1

Planet	Average distance from sun (km)	Scale distance from sun (cm)
Mercury	58 000 000	
Venus	108 000 000	
Earth	150 000 000	
Mars	229 000 000	
Jupiter	777 000 000	
Saturn	1 426 000 000	
Uranus	2 876 000 000	
Neptune	4 490 000 000	
Pluto	5 914 000 000	
Scale of distances		

NAME _____ DATE _____ CLASS _____

Chapter 24
LABORATORY MANUAL

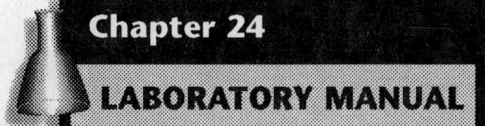

Star Colors 68

In 1665, Isaac Newton demonstrated that sunlight was composed of many colors. Today the spectra of a star is one of the most important tools scientists use to determine the star's surface temperature and composition. The Draper system of spectral classification is used in this activity.

Strategy
You will define the term *star*.
You will observe and record star colors.
You will classify stars based on their color.

Materials
binoculars or telescope (optional)
graph paper

Star Classification Chart
Table 68-1

Star spectral type	Color	Surface temperature (K)
M	red	2000–4000
K	red to orange	3500–5000
G	yellow	5000–6000
F	yellow-white	6000–7500
A	white	9000
B	bluish-white	11 000–25 000
O	bluish-white	60 000

Procedure
1. On a clear, bright night observe the stars with your eyes or with the binoculars or telescope.
2. Use some landmarks and divide the sky into four sections. Label the landmarks in the diagram under Data and Observations.
3. Observe and record the color of each star in each section. Record your observations on your diagram under Data and Observations.
4. Compile your data showing the star color, class, and number of stars in each section in a table. Set up your table on one end of your graph paper.
5. Draw a bar graph showing the star classes and the number of stars in each class under the table on the graph paper.

Data and Observations
Diagram night sky here.

Questions and Conclusions

1. What property did you use to classify a celestial body as a star? _____
_____
_____

2. Which star class is the most abundant? _____
_____

3. Which star class does our sun belong to? _____

4. What is the surface temperature of our sun? _____

5. The temperature of stars is given in Kelvins. Changing from the Celsius scale to the Kelvin scale is very easy: K = °C + 273°. What is the temperature of the sun in Celsius degrees?
_____

Strategy Check

_____ Can you define the term *star*?

_____ Can you observe and record the colors of the stars?

_____ Can you classify stars based on their color?

Chapter 24
LABORATORY MANUAL
Star Trails 69

As Earth rotates on its axis, the stars appear to move also. The north star, Polaris, is a fixed reference point because it is almost directly above the north pole of Earth's axis of rotation. The pole position does not appear to move.

Strategy
You will photograph Polaris in a time exposure.
You will determine how many degrees Earth has rotated during the time exposure.

Materials
camera with time exposure paper (tracing)
compass (drawing) protractor
film (black and white) tripod or support for camera

Procedure
1. Load the camera and mount it on the tripod.

2. On a clear, moonless night, set up the camera outside. Aim the camera so that Polaris is in the center of the viewing field.

3. Set the focus on infinity and open the shutter for a time exposure. Record the time and the landmark that is right under Polaris in Table 69-1.

4. Three hours later, close the shutter. Record the landmark that is under Polaris in Table 69-1. Have the film developed. Explain to the developer what you photographed, and ask for special care in the developing.

5. Trace several of the arcs on your developed print on the tracing paper. Be sure to include the arc traced by Polaris. Label the end points.

6. Use the compass to determine the center of the circle of which the arc of Polaris is a part. Mark the center of the circle with a dot.

7. Draw a line from the center of the circle made by Polaris to the ends of five star curves you traced. Measure the angles between each pair of lines with a protractor. Record each angle in Table 69-2.

Data and Observations
Table 69-1

	Landmark
Start	
Finish	

Table 69-2

Star pairs	Angle (°)
Polaris and Star 1	
Polaris and Star 2	
Polaris and Star 3	
Polaris and Star 4	
Polaris and Star 5	

Questions and Conclusions

1. Did the landmarks change? _____ In what direction do the stars appear to move?
   _____

2. What does your print show? _____
   _____

3. What is the central point in the picture? _____
   Explain. _____
   _____

4. How far did the stars appear to move per hour in degrees? _____

5. How long does it take Earth to make one complete rotation based on your average arc?
   _____

6. How long could you have left the shutter open? _____ Explain.
   _____
   _____

7. Do the stars actually move as the print seems to prove? _____ Explain.
   _____
   _____

8. If the shutter had been left open for 4 hours, how many degrees would Earth have rotated?
   _____

Strategy Check

_____ Can you photograph Polaris?

_____ Can you determine how far Earth rotates during a time exposure?

NAME _____ DATE _____ CLASS _____

Chapter 24
LABORATORY MANUAL
• Star Positions 70

When you watch the stars on a clear night, do you get the impression that you are in an upside-down bowl? The ancient Greeks believed that the stars were fixed to a clear bowl that slowly rotated around Earth. Although today we know that Earth rotates, the celestial sphere is still a good model to use to locate stars and other celestial bodies.

Strategy
You will construct a model of the north celestial hemisphere.
You will plot the stars on the celestial sphere.

Materials
globe (mounted)
hemisphere (clear plastic or terrarium top)
pen (felt-tip)
string to go around celestial equator

Procedure
1. The celestial sphere appears to move around a line that is an extension of Earth's axis. The north and south celestial poles are the points where Earth's geographic axis intersects the celestial sphere; see Figure 70-1. Label the north celestial pole with a dot on the inside of the hemisphere.

2. The celestial equator is the intersection of a plane that passes through Earth's equator and the celestial sphere. Place the clear hemisphere over the globe so that the North Pole and the north celestial pole are in line. Mark the celestial equator on the hemisphere. The celestial equator is 90° from the celestial poles; see Figure 70-1.

3. Planes comparable to latitude on Earth are called *declination* on the celestial sphere. Positions north of the celestial equator are called *plus declination* and measured in degrees. Positions south of the celestial equator are called *minus declination*, also measured in degrees.

4. The celestial circle that corresponds to the Prime Meridian of longitude on Earth is called *right ascension*. Right ascension is measured from the point where the sun crosses the celestial equator about March 21 (the Vernal equinox).

5. Right ascension is measured in hours, minutes, and seconds. 15 degrees of arc on the equator equals 1 hour. Take a length of string and measure the distance around the celestial equator in centimeters. Record. Divide this distance by 24. Measure and mark these spaces around the celestial equator. Each mark represents 1 hour. Start at the Prime Meridian and move eastward around the celestial equator; see Figure 70-1.

6. Now you have a grid system similar to latitude and longitude.

7. Map the locations of the following stars on the celestial sphere.

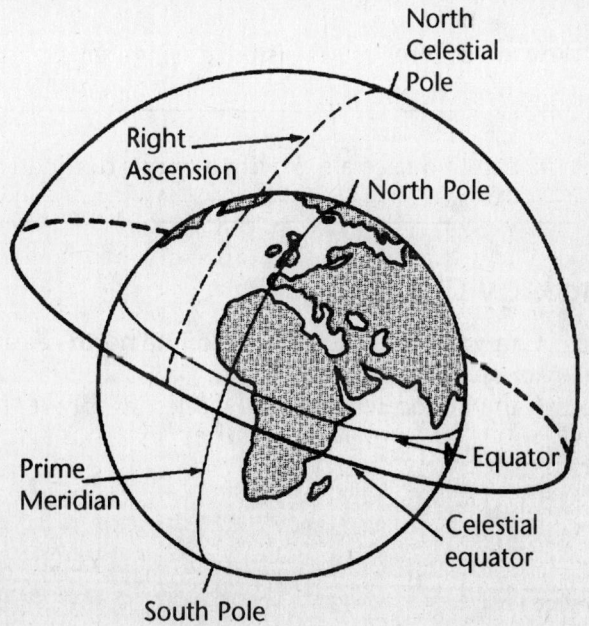

FIGURE 70-1

Copyright © Glencoe/McGraw-Hill, a division of the McGraw-Hill Companies, Inc.

175

Table 70-1

Common name	Scientific name	R.A. hr	R.A. min	Dec. (°)
Vega	Lyrae	18	35	38
Arcturus	Bootes	14	13	19
Altair	Aquilae	19	48	8
Betelgeuse	Orionis	05	52	7
Aldebaran	Tauri	04	33	16
Deneb	Cygni	20	40	45
Regulus	Leonis	10	06	12
Castor	Geminorum	07	31	32

Data and Observations

Celestial equator = _____ cm

Questions and Conclusions

1. How is right ascension like longitude? _____
   How is it different? _____

2. Compare declination to latitude. _____
   _____

3. What does the vernal equinox on the celestial sphere correspond to on geographic maps?
   _____

4. Why are different stars visible during the year? _____
   _____

5. Why can't you see a star with a minus declination from the northern hemisphere? _____
   _____

Strategy Check

_____ Can you construct a model of the north celestial hemisphere?

_____ Can you locate stars on the celestial sphere?